Reflections From The Light Of Christ:
Five Quaker Classics

by
James R. Newby

RICHMOND
INDIANA

Published by
Friends United Press
Richmond, IN 47374

Copyright, 1980
by
Friends United Press

Library of Congress Number — 80-7477
I.S.B.N. 0-9134-8-55-7

Printed in the United States of America
by
Prinit Press, Dublin, IN 47335

*For My Parents
Richard and Doris Newby
With Love and Appreciation*

Contents

Foreword by D. Elton Trueblood................... *vii*
Preface... *xi*
1. William Penn: Follower Of The Light Of Christ...... 1
    Fruits Of Solitude
2. John Woolman: Apostle Of Human Freedom...... 25
    The Journal
3. Hannah Whitall Smith:
    Teacher Of The Interior Life.................... 43
    The Christian's Secret Of A Happy Life
4. Rufus Jones: Interpreter Of The Inward Way...... 65
    The Double Search, and Others
5. Thomas Kelly: Prophet Of Spiritual Religion...... 89
    A Testament Of Devotion

FOREWORD

The list of genuine classics of devotion is inevitably a short one, but, however short the list may be, it always includes a number of Quaker writings. For example, it is difficult to find a list of devotional classics, whatever the national or denominational source, that does not call attention to *The Journal of John Woolman.* It is strange but true that perceptive readers turn regularly to Quaker writers for an understanding of the deepest character of the inner life.

The fact that Quakers are now, and always have been, a tiny minority of the total population has not prevented seekers of many sorts from turning to the insights of George Fox, especially when, in dealing with the reality of God, he sought to turn people away from "knowledge about" to "acquaintance with" the Source of their being. Any sensitive hearer, of any generation, has a good chance of being reached inwardly by the words of Fox when he said, "You will say, *Christ saith this and the apostles say this; but what canst thou say?* Art thou a child of Light, and hast thou walked in the Light, and what thou speakest, is it inwardly from God?" The question is so much to the point that we can understand why Thomas Carlyle termed the beginning of the public ministry of Fox "the greatest incident in modern history." Carlyle was operating upon the belief that, however significant outward events may be, what occurs in the inner life of a people is of primary importance.

The words of Isaac Penington are even more penetrating than those of Fox. He was one of the persons who, according to William Penn, "were changed men themselves before they went about to change others." Penington, writing often in prison, saw vividly that the ultimate ground of certainty lies in direct personal experience. "We can truly say concerning the Scriptures," he wrote, "that now we believe not so much because of the relation of things concerning Christ which we have found in them, but because we have seen and received the thing which the Scriptures speak of."

The witness of Robert Barclay has been a source of strength to great numbers outside as well as inside the Society of Friends, especially in his account of how the Living God reached him so mightily that he became the chief human instrument in ending religious imprisonment in Great Britain. Though an undoubted intellectual, Barclay reported that his faith was established "not by strength of arguments, or by a particular disquisition of each doctrine, and convincement of my understanding thereby,... but by secretly being reached by this life."

Such men as Fox, Penington and Barclay are, by any reasonable standard, true giants and, accordingly, they belong to the Church Universal. Their brilliant insights, far from being the guarded possessions of a sect, belong to all who are willing to listen. Since true ecumenicity is seen best in the act of sharing, it is right that the genuine classics of any particular group should be made available to others. This is what James Newby is attempting to accomplish in this beautiful book. He proposes to introduce the thoughtful reader, whatever his persuasion, to five giants, all of whom belong both to Friends and to the larger community of faith. In this laborious task, Mr. Newby is performing a valuable and overdue service. I am grateful to him, and commend his book to seekers everywhere.

D. Elton Trueblood

PREFACE

In the course of studying the history of the People called Quakers, two major contributions come into prominence. On the one hand, Friends are known for their active social concern. Since their beginning 325 years ago, the story of Friends attacking a series of social evils has been a thrilling one. The most notable of these are the recognition of the evil of human slavery, the effort to care for the mentally ill without cruelty, the change in attitude toward prisoners, from inhuman to human treatment, and the continuous effort to work for peaceful solutions to problems between individuals, groups and nations. This concern for the social well-being of humankind is a heritage in which Friends take satisfaction, and one which continues today.

At the same time that Quakers have been known for their attacks upon various forms of oppression, they have been equally known for their cultivation of the inner life of devotion. Those who suppose that the People called Quakers are just an ethical culture society miss the point. If Friends were merely that they would have died long ago. Because there have been inward springs, the fountains have continued to flow. Some of these are muddied because of a lack of understanding concerning the Quaker spiritual roots, but, for the most part, they have never ceased to emphasize the inner spring. No other religious group has been as much given to the keeping of journals, most of which emphasize the Divine/Human encounter. Though generally people know about the Quaker spiritual classics, or they know about their service in the world, Quakers are known so much for both of these emphases that it is impossible to know which is the major one. Since this double priority is the most striking aspect of Quakers, their power lies in the fact that they stress both equally. This witness to the necessity of keeping these two enterprises together is the chief message Friends are able to give to the world. Not only *can* they go together, but they *must* go together. They are necessary for each other if there is to be a wholistic Christian faith. If we have only the emphasis on the inner life of devotion. without social concern, we become self-centered and complacent. On the other hand, if we have only active social concern without the sensitivity which comes from within, we become arrogant and judgmental. Our hope lies in holding the inner spring and the outer fountain together. If either one is absent, spiritual death is certain to ensue.

This volume is a study of some of the best Quaker Classics of devotion, the fruits of one half of this double priority. In the chapters which follow I shall discuss persons who have been, in a peculiar degree, prophets of the soul by virtue of their own direct experience. Out of the experience of the Divine in their lives, these spiritual geniuses have produced the literature of witness, which has played an important part in the lives of millions, regardless of labels. Since their beginning in 1652, Friends have sought to recover spiritual religion by direct communion with God, through the inner light of Jesus Christ. George Fox, the founder of the Quaker movement, writes of his purpose for sharing his spiritual experiences in the opening sentence of his *Journal*: "That all may know the dealings of the Lord with me, and the various exercises, trials, and troubles through which he led me..." Out of a like concern, John Woolman shares his reason for writing his *Journal*: "I have often felt a motion of love to leave some hints in writing of my experience of the goodness of God, and now, in the thirty-sixth year of my age, I begin this work."

Quakers have, compared to their size, produced a disproportionate number of writings on the inner life. It is something of a revelation to realize that Hannah Whitall Smith's classic, *The Christian's Secret Of A Happy Life*, has actually been purchased by more than two million readers. Mrs. Smith and, indeed, all of the classic Quaker writers have been ecumenical in the sense that each has attracted a large following in the general intellectual and spiritual community. Likewise, Thomas Kelly's book, *A Testament of Devotion*, has reached vastly more non-Quakers than Quakers, and in his recent collection of *The Doubleday Devotional Classics*, Dr. Glenn Hinson from Southern Seminary selected nine volumes, four of which are produced by Quaker authors. If we are looking for an explanation of this phenomenon, I believe that we can find one. Although individual Christian mysticism is good, group mysticism is even more powerful. The Quaker classics have had a more fertile ground in which to develop than is usually found in other Christian settings. The emphasis upon direct experience in a social silence, has given the seed of God within these authors an extraordinary fertile setting in which to grow.

Since the authors of the Quaker classics are Christian mystics, it is important to define what is meant by a Quaker conception of mysticism. Since this term is often shrouded in confusion, clarity of thinking is important. Quakers understand Basic Christian Mysticism to be the effort to follow the guiding Hand of God through the Inner Light of Jesus Christ. It follows, then, that a mystic, in the Quaker sense, is a person who has cultivated, with strenuous care and discipline, a soul attuned to the "still small voice" of the Living Christ. The Quaker mystic experiences times when his or her life is surrounded by a larger life beyond and within, fulfilling the basic search for a Divine/Human encounter. The Quaker classics of devotion exemplify this definition.

One of the worst of our current intellectual dangers is our temporal snobbishness. Because we suppose that if something is a few years old it has, for that reason, nothing to say to us, we ask of a book, not whether what is said is true, but the date at which it was produced. By this arrogance we become bound to the passing moment, unable to experience the liberation of the printed word through the centuries. An important lesson for us to learn is that truth is independent of the time when it is written. Spiritual classics are possible because persons are basically alike in all times and places. There is, accordingly, funded experience. Consequently, such a man as William Penn has still much to teach us. We shall always have need of his kind of religious realism and common sense. The simple Quaker prophet, John Woolman, can continue to express the ideal Christian life through the words of his timeless *Journal.* We shall never reach a period when the words of the teacher of the interior life, Hannah Whitall Smith, can not bring new light to our earthly paths. Rufus Jones, through his understanding of the conjunct life and interpretation of the inward way, can forever lift our hearts to the higher regions of the spirit. And Thomas Kelly, with his thoughts on Holy Obedience, can always provide us with instruction on how to order our lives around the Divine Center. In spite of the many changes which our world has witnessed over the course of three centuries, the words in the Quaker classics are still of primary importance to us.

Dr. Willard L. Sperry, former Dean of Harvard

Divinity School, has provided a model throughout the writing of this book. In his volume, *Strangers and Pilgrims,* he introduces readers to the life and works of six persons who have made permanent contributions to the spiritual life by their dateless writings. In this beautiful book Dean Sperry includes, Saint Augustine, Saint Francis of Assisi, Thomas a Kempis, the author of *The Theologia Germanica,* Brother Lawrence, and John Woolman. The only place in which my book overlaps his, is in the treatment of John Woolman, a name which may be expected to appear in all such collections. Sperry's work has meant more to me because he was the inspiration of my teacher, Elton Trueblood, and was, indeed, the one who taught my mentor to soak himself in the great models.

Richmond, Indiana
Thanksgiving, 1979　　　　　　　　　　James R. Newby

Chapter I

William Penn: Follower Of The Light Of Christ

"... *There is not the man living, no, nor recently dead, that could put, with so lovely a spirit, so much honest, kind wisdom into words.*"
— Robert Louis Stevenson

In December of 1879, Robert Louis Stevenson walked the streets of San Francisco lonely and discouraged, following a serious bout with an illness that had left him weak and without hope. As he wandered among the little shops of this City by the Bay, he entered a second-hand book store, and while browsing at random, came across a copy of William Penn's *Fruits Of Solitude*. Little did he suspect, at that moment, that he was about to purchase a piece of literature which would change his life almost completely. Taking Penn's little classic home, he read it and was immediately lifted with a strong sense of hope. Later he was to write about this important life changing event as he parted with his personal copy of this book, hoping to better the life of his dear friend, Horatio F. Brown:

> If ever in all my 'human conduct' I have done a better thing to any fellow creature than handing on to you this sweet, dignified, and wholesome book, I know I shall hear of it on the last day. To write a book like this were impossible; at least one can hand it on, with a wrench, one to another. My wife cries out and my own heart misgives me, but still — here it is.

And in a later note to the same correspondent:

> I hope, if you get thus far, you will know what an invaluable present I have made you. Even the copy was dear to me, printed in the colony that Penn established, and carried in my pocket all about the San Francisco streets, read in street-cars and ferry boats, when I was sick unto death, and found in all times and places a peaceful and sweet companion.

The impact of William Penn upon the life of Robert Louis Stevenson is clear and unmistakable. Following his encounter with *Fruits Of Solitude,* Stevenson's whole moral philosophy was tinged with Penn's spiritual realism, and permeated throughout with his sense of hope. There is evidence that this prolific author wanted to make Penn and his classic the subject of one of his critical essays, but sickness prevented the completion of this dream. However, even though he never found the opportunity to write an essay about the book which he loved so much, he, nevertheless, revealed the benificent influence of Penn in much that he wrote after his encounter with this Quaker classic.

A concrete result of Stevenson's discovery of a hitherto unknown classic, was his own production of religious literature, which seems certain also to endure. During his residence in the South Seas, in the years immediately preceding his untimely death, Stevenson produced prayers which are greatly prized by those who are fortunate enough to know them. The following is an example:

> Aid us, it if be thy will, in our concerns. Have mercy on this land and innocent people. Help them who this day contend in disappointment with their frailties. Bless our family, bless our forest house, bless our island helpers. Thou who hast made for us this place of ease and hope, accept and inflame our gratitude; help us to repay, in service one to another, the debt of thine unmerited benefits and mercies, so that, when the period of our stewardship draws to a conclusion, when the windows begin to be darkened, when the

bond of the family is to be loosed, there shall be no bitterness of remorse in our farewells.

Robert Louis Stevenson discovered an often neglected quality of William Penn within the pages of this timeless classic. This inward aspect of his life is often overlooked, since in the public estimation he is chiefly a colonist and statesman. Nearly every literate person knows the name of Penn, but millions do not know him as a serious author on the inner life of the Spirit. Though he is by far the best known Quaker who has ever lived, he is "best known" because of his political genius, and not because of what he wrote.

The inner side of this famous man found literary expression in *Fruits Of Solitude*. Dissatisfied with a faith that limited itself to the outward law of God, with no attention given to the inward grace of God, Penn became, at an early age, a convinced Friend, determined to go beyond external authorities to a religion of inward life and power. In response to the religious formalism of Seventeenth Century England, William Penn challenged his contemporaries to think in the spirit of Basic Christianity.

... It is a conformity of mind and practice to the will of God, in all holiness of conversation, according to the dictates of this Divine Principle of Light and Life in the soul which denotes a person truly a child of God.

Penn fully believed that he was called to bear witness to this eternal word within the soul, and in his lifetime he did more than any other Friend to carry out this important mission.

Sometimes in his home in Sussex, and sometimes in hiding in the heart of London, William Penn was living, in 1690, in forced retirement. This man of political and religious activity had been stripped of his control over his beloved colony in America, and suspected of disloyalty by King William. Because Penn had had a close relationship with King James II, in the days immediately before the "Grand and Glorious Revolution," Penn's political influence fell with the House of Stuart. Alone and isolated from the driving activity of the world, Penn found himself under what amounted to house arrest. He was actually suspected of being a Jesuit in disguise. His forced retirement, however, became, in the end, a genuine blessing.

What events had transpired in the life of William Penn to bring him to this world of solitude? How was his life formed? Who were the people and what were the influences of the time that molded this man who has been called "the first of the Quaker moralists?"

William Penn was born into what Alfred North Whitehead has called "The Century Of Genius." His date of birth, October 14, 1644, occurred three months after the battle of Marston Moor, which was the decisive battle in the English Civil War. He was four years old when Charles was executed. King Charles had been more than just a monarch to the members of the Penn family, for they had known their King personally. His death was viewed by the Penns, not only as a violation of the dignity of England, but also as a deep personal loss.

Since Sir William Penn Sr. was a naval man, whose duty it was to guard England at sea against foreign agressors, he did not become involved in the contest over the English flag at home. His allegiance was changed a number of times — from Charles I, to Parliament, to Cromwell, to Charles II. There can be little doubt, however, that William Penn Sr. supported the restoration of the Stuarts to the throne, since, after he was elected a member of Parliament, he was one of the representatives that were sent to bring Charles II back from his exile in Holland.

Young William began his formal education at Chigwell School which was well known for its orthodox influences. It was sometime during the last few months at this school that he experienced his first religious discovery of which there is any record. Catherine Owens Peare relates this incident in her beautifully written, and historically important biography on Penn:

> In a moment of solitude, perhaps in an attitude of prayer, he felt a sudden inward peace, an enlightening of himself and a brightening of the room around him. It was his discovery of God, a thing which must always be personal. Through all the forms, catechisms, memorized prayers and required readings had penetrated a light, a knowing, a direct communication with the divine which would never be lost.[1]

After experiencing failure on a mission to the West Indies, the elder Penn was arrested and placed in the Tower of London, but it was a brief imprisonment, lasting only five weeks. Following his release, the Admiral took his family to Ireland, to the Castle and Manor of Macroom. Son William had been taken out of Chigwell, his education now being entrusted to a private tutor. His first contact with the People called Quakers came at the age of 12 during his stay in Ireland. In his father's home in the County of Cork, he heard Thomas Loe, one of the traveling Quaker preachers. This contact with Loe greatly impressed young William, and can now be seen as the event which started a course of action that would make this junior aristocrat a great Quaker leader.

At the age of 16, William Penn was sent to Christ Church College, Oxford. His father had moved back to London in March of 1660, and was appointed to a seat in the new convention Parliament. Young William made a good adjustment in his first year at college, but the second year was turning out very different. During this time England was just beginning the restoration, and persecution of the Puritan Sects was gaining momentum. The Anglican Church was being re-established as the ONLY church of the land. William Penn found himself protesting the new rigid regulations and persecution, and he refused to attend chapel services, going instead to hear lectures by Dr. John Owen who had been dismissed from his position as Dean of Christ Church because of his Puritan sympathies. Penn was becoming, by Seventeenth Century standards, a heretic, and by March of 1662 he was expelled from Oxford.

Following this severe blow to his prestige, Admiral Penn sent his son to France to complete his education. After a year and a half the young Penn returned to England, but not until he had had his first experience in non-violence. He relates this incident as follows:

> I was once myself in France . . . set upon about eleven at night, as I was walking to my lodging, by a person that way-laid me, with his naked sword in his hand, who demanded satisfaction of me for taking no notice of him, at a time when he civilly saluted me with his hat; tho' the truth was, I saw him not when he did it. I will suppose he had killed me, for he made several passes at me, or I in my defence had killed him, when I disarmed him (as the Earl of Crawford's servant saw, that was by). I ask any man of understanding or conscience, if the whole ceremony were worth the life of a man, considering the dignity of the nature, and the importance of the life of man, both with respect to God his creator, himself, and the benefit of civil society?"[2]

Penn could not accept the silly law that stated the doffing of a hat was worth a man's life. He was becoming sensitized to the cruelty of man's inhumanity to man, and by God's grace, this incident in France came to an end without bloodshed.

While in France, Penn was absorbed into the thinking of Amyraut, which was the theological atmosphere of Saumur where he went to school. As Catherine Peare states: "He had arrived carrying within himself a growing accumulation of religious experiences; he remained to have those experiences verified and amplified by a doctrine of morality based upon free will guided by that of God in every man."[3]

When he returned to London, Penn studied law at Lincoln's Inn, but later went to Ireland to manage his father's estates. It was during this time in Ireland that he heard Thomas Loe for a second time, and as a result became a convinced Friend. Penn was 22 years old when he became a Quaker, and when his father heard of his new affiliation, he was incensed. At this point in his son's life, however, there was nothing he could do to stop what he considered to be "Quaker foolishness."

From this time on, the life of William Penn is seen as a struggle for religious freedom, and more specifically Quaker freedom. His new non-conformity caused him imprisonments, but this did not break his spirit; if anything they strengthened it. His faith was an anvil which wore out many hammers. One of the finest pieces of prison literature ever produced comes from the hand of Penn while in the tower of London, entitled, *No Cross, No Crown*. Alone and isolated at the age of 24, surrounded in the drab atmosphere of a dirty prison cell, Penn was able to rise to great heights spiritually. The depressing circumstances from without did not weaken his spirit within, and the following words, penned during this experience of prison life, express the remarkable fortitude of this witness for Christ: "The Lamp the Lord has lighted is not utterly extinct."[4] While his outward environment sought to extinguish his hope, he was given new strength within, and this spiritual power enabled him to see his faith as an inward discipline: "Taking up the cross of Jesus is a more interior exercise; it is the circumspection and discipline of the soul in conformity to the divine mind therein revealed."[5]

Like *No Cross, No Crown*, which was Penn's first major piece of writing, *Fruits of Solitude* can be considered an affiliate to the many formidable volumes which can be classified under the genre of prison literature, since he was under house arrest when these small books were produced.[6] Here he is part of a great tradition of prison authors, to which Socrates, Boethius, the Apostle Paul, John Bunyan and Dietrich Bonhoeffer all belong. Even Daniel Defoe wrote in prison from 1704-1713, starting a set of essays which may be regarded as a forerunner of the "Tatler" and "Spectator." The prison cell has, indeed, been the setting out of which many prolific authors have written some of their best works, and it has often been the fertile ground of Christian reform, where the seeds of renewal are planted within an individual, and, consequently, a society. In the words of St. Augustine, "One loving spirit sets another on fire," and when in the solitude of a prison cell, history has shown that individual fires are provided a conducive opportunity to be kindled.

After twenty years of patient work for religious freedom in England, Penn was becoming discouraged, and wrote in 1680: "There is no hope in England, the deaf adder cannot be charmed." He began to look abroad for an opportunity to demonstrate to the world how a Christian society should be governed. He yearned for a place where he could conduct his Holy Experiment.

In 1681 Penn's dream came true. Charles II owed Penn's father a large debt, which he chose to pay by giving son William a large section of land in America, now known as Pennsylvania. With the granting of this land Penn was now free to establish a government in his own colony that would allow for religious toleration and where the people would govern in a democracy. He wrote his Frame of Government for the new colony in 1682 with his intentions for this adventure being spelled out in a letter to some Friends in Ireland:

> As my understanding and inclination have been much directed to observe and reprove mischiefs in government, so it is now put into my power to settle one. For the matters of liberty and privilege I propose that which is extraordinary, and to leave myself and successors no power of doing mischief, that the will of

one man may not hinder the good of a whole country.

Pennsylvania, which Penn wanted to call New Wales, was a constant burden, since the legal and financial problems associated with the proprietorship of a colony kept him in England for extended periods of time. However, he was certainly needed in England as much as in America, especially by members of his Religious Society. Many Friends were imprisoned, and the only hope for their release lay in the close association William Penn had with King James. In 1686 the King finally issued a pardon to Quakers, and nearly 1,300 Friends left the confines of prison. Within the following two years, just prior to the "Grand and Glorious Revolution," King James also issued two general Acts of Indulgence. Without the work of Penn this would never have happened.

William Penn was forced into inactivity in 1690, but his mind was too active to remain idle. This time of liberation from the burdens of political life gave him an opportunity to write. During these years Penn produced two of his most famous pieces — *Some Fruits Of Solitude* and *Essay On The Peace Of Europe*. These two selections from the hand of Penn, which are completely different in composition and message, demonstrate the amazing flexibility of mind that he possessed, and the way in which he was able to combine both the inward and outward elements of his faith. Here was a man who was outwardly concerned for the peace of the world and developed a specific plan for world order, yet he stayed close enough to the inward springs of spiritual nourishment to be able to produce a beautiful piece of devotional literature.

The style of *Fruits Of Solitude* reveals the French literary influence of Penn's day. Using the trenchant sentence which La Rochefoucauld made famous, Penn writes straight to the mark, making his sentences vivid and intense, with nothing elaborated. There had developed in France a feeling that the phrase must be made simple to produce a sharp and precise effect, and the great Duke of La Rochefoucauld popularized this style. The Duke's *Maximes* were published in Paris in 1665, and they immediately became a model of all sententious and oracular aphorisms. In 1687, the *Pensees* of Pascal were issued and were of the same compact style. This literary influence was most assuredly at work on Penn while he wrote *Fruits of Solitude,* but one major difference must be noted between him and his model La Rochefoucauld. Where La Rochefoucauld is the living spirit of negativism, Penn is the dynamic spokesman of hope and optimism. Life was not bitter for Penn, and throughout his "Maxims and Reflections" he combats the cynical attitude which his literary model perpetuated.

Although his writing style reflects what was vogue during this time, the concerns of which he speaks and the spiritual messages he relates are his own. Since the fruits are grown in his own orchard, he truly believes what he says, and wants others to see it and believe it. It is hard to imagine an area of life which this book does not cover, and if there is one weakness in this writing it is because Penn has tried to cover too much in too little space. However, this was the style he sought to emulate, and as John Clifford writes in the Introduction to the 1905 edition of *Some Fruits,* this book "is a summing up and classifying of the vast results of human experience by an expert in the art and science of living, expressed with great simplicity and naturalness in compact, cogent and clear English."[7]

Penn was forty-nine years old when this volume was published. He had already lived a full and active existence in the service of his God and country and at this two-thirds interval in his life he was able, in his own words, to take "a view of himself and the world, and observe wherein he hath hit and missed the mark; what might have been done, what mended, and what avoided in his Human Conduct..."[8] His faithful companion and spiritual father George Fox died in 1691, and his dear friend Robert Barclay had died in 1690. These deaths marked the end of the first forty years of Quakerism, and the end of what Elton Trueblood has called "The Quaker Explosion." The time had come in Penn's personal history to reflect on his life and generate a new hope for his future. Through the discipline of writing, his solitude became fruitful.

William Penn writes in the Preface to *Some Fruits Of Solitude:* "There is nothing of which we are apt to be so lavish as of time, and about which we ought to be more solicitous; since without it we can do nothing in this world. Time is what we want most, but what, alas! we use worst; and for which God will certainly most strictly reckon with us, when time shall be no more." With these moving words on the discipline of time, Penn immediately presses us to enter the mystical world of self-awareness: "... till we are persuaded to stop and step a little aside, out of the noisy crowd and incumbering hurry of the world, and calmly take a prospect of things, it will be impossible we should be able to make a right judgment of ourselves or know our own misery..." Penn discovered that this must be the first step in developing an inner life of devotion, for by stepping out of the noisy mass of humanity, he was able to think and meditate on the condition of his spiritual self, a process through which all pilgrims must go. He concerns himself with the neglect of this inner world, and his words speak to our spiritual condition today, just as they spoke to the condition of Seventeenth Century England. We do not know ourselves, the structure of our minds, or the Divine Spark within us, just waiting to break forth if only properly nourished in the deeper regions of the spirit. The words of William Penn speak to the condition of all persons regardless of time, since throughout the history of the world attention to the development of the world within has not been actively sought, mainly because the immediate reality of the Living Christ is not outwardly seen, and therefore difficult for our material minds to understand. But although it is not outwardly seen, this Spirit is inwardly felt, and is the source of our larger visions and hopes, all of which separate humanity from the rest of God's Kingdom. It is this need for inner penetration that so concerned William Penn, and is the main theme of all his classics on the inner life of devotion. The human heart will forever be in need of his gentle proddings to turn inward, and in the words which follow Penn further instructs his students on this basic ingredient of spiritual religion:

> The Light of Christ Within, who is the light of the world, (and so a light to you, that tells you the truth of your condition,) leads all, that take heed unto it, out of darkness into God's marvellous light. For light grows upon the obedient; it is 'sown for the righteous,' and their way is a shining light, that shines forth more and more to the perfect day. Wherefore, O friends, TURN IN, TURN IN, I beseech you; where there is the poison there is the antidote. There you want Christ and there you must find Him; and blessed be God there you may find Him.[9]

One touches in these words the very secret of Christian mysticism, that in the inner life itself, not in the outside material world, lies the hope of humankind. This mystical awareness of Penn was formed during a tumultuous time in the history of England, and finding no spiritual nourishment from the outward forms of religious teaching, he became hostile toward them. He sought a direct experience with God, and through the teaching of George Fox, Penn moved from being a seeker, to one who had found. This uneducated rustic from Northern England became Penn's spiritual father, and together they were able to preach, and to teach seekers of all persuasions the "good news" of the Living

Light of Jesus Christ. The courtly Penn and the unsophisticated Fox made a team, that when fused produced greatness. Out of this close relationship with the founder of the People called Quakers, he wrote this moving epitaph:
> Many sons have done virtuously in this day; but dear George, thou excellest them all.[10]

Through the teaching of Fox, Penn was brought to the simple, basic understanding of the Christian faith, that "To be like Christ . . . is to be a Christian." In the person of George Fox, William Penn saw this teaching exemplified, and he also received a visionary hope of a new reformation.

John Greenleaf Whittier has written, "Quakerism . . . as interpreted by Penn and Barclay, is the most liberal and catholic of faiths." For Penn, Seventeenth Century Quakerism was nothing less than "Primitive Christianity Revived." The People called Quakers began as a movement that transcended sectarian borders, and Penn, through his leadership, led this new found people to a much larger vision of greatness than was usually found in the Protestant thinking of his day. This new faith was a religion of experience that went beyond the confines of a sect. It was not an intellectual process, but a way of life. It was not a system of thought or a set of dogmas, but a vital spiritual religion, which he understood as Basic Christianity. In the words which follow, Penn emphasizes the ecumenicity of this exciting faith:
> The humble, meek, merciful, just, pious, and devout souls, are everywhere of one religion; and when death has taken off the mask, they will know one another, though the divers liveries they wear here make them strangers.[11]

The founder of Pennsylvania was one of those rare personalities through which the Spirit of God was able to reach out and feed the spiritually hungry. The brief but deeply moving passages in *Some Fruits of Solitude* witness to the creative mind and sensitive spirit of this practical Christian mystic. We can detect one of the reasons why he was such a bountiful harvester for Christ when we read his words on the virtues of discipline and hard work in the life of the family and individual:

> If thou wouldst be happy and easie in thy family, above all things observe discipline . . .
> Everyone in it should know their duty; and there should be a time and place for everything; and whatever else is done or omitted, be sure to begin and end with God . . . .[12]

Though these are words that may sound unfamiliar to a generation that has been reared to believe that discipline means an end to freedom, Penn knew that quite the opposite is actually true. He understood that if persons are to be truly free, then they must so discipline their lives as to take full advantage of the tremendous opportunities available to them. It is only by discipline that one is able to read and thus experience mind expanding knowledge. It is only by discipline that one is able to play the piano or any other musical instrument, and thus experience the joy of producing melody. It is only by disciplining the hours in one's day that he is able to accomplish his work. And it was only through discipline that Penn was able to write so beautifully. He knew that the absolutely free individual is bound by his own freedom, and attributes to the death of his own creative humanity.

Penn's concern for the development of a disciplined spirit would not only produce harmony in the individual and family, but would temper our life-style as well. Two-hundred and eighty-seven years ago, William Penn warned of the misuse of our physical environment, and in the words which follow he sounds amazingly contemporary as he pleads for moderation in the use of our God-given material wealth:

> The most common things are the most useful; which shews both the wisdom and goodness of the great Lord of the family of the world.... What therefore he has made rare, don't thou use too commonly: lest thou shouldest invert the use and order of things; become wanton and voluptuous; and thy blessings prove a curse.... Let nothing be lost, said our Saviour. But that is lost that is misused....[13]

These prophetic words of Penn awaken our moral sense to the destructiveness of our ways, and they echo the Quaker testimony on Simplicity, which promotes fullness of life without the clutter of possessions. The striving for material wealth and the destruction of the earth causes unnecessary burdens upon humankind, and eventually leads to the neglect of the spiritual life. Penn urges simple tastes in our manner of living that help us to abolish destructive competition, and encourage the value of self-denial.

In a life of complexity, a person is constantly being challenged with many ends for which to live, and many values for which to strive. In *Fruits of Solitude* Penn helps us to see lesser and lower ones falling into place under wider and higher ones. He is an eternal optimist who believed that as persons become sensitive to God's leading, they discover that life is more than the daily struggles to acquire more material things, and more a matter of giving themselves to spiritual values. Penn sought to sensitize persons to this inward leading, and always witnessed to the joy of being obedient to the Christ Within.

Within the pages of this Quaker Classic, we quickly discover that the writing of William Penn has a strength without harshness, a sternness without severity, and a tenderness without appearing weak. This rare ability is best expressed in the words which follow as he shares his thoughts on the subject of spiritual religion, and pours out the treasures of his soul, which obviously sprung from a faith that was experiential:

Religion is the fear of God, and its demonstration good works; and faith is the root of both: for without faith we cannot please God, nor can we fear what we do not believe . . .

Let us today, therefore, hear his voice, and not harden our hearts; who speaks to us many ways: in the Scriptures, in our hearts, by his servants and his providences: and the sum of all is HOLINESS AND CHARITY . . .

For serving God concerns the frame of our spirits, in the whole course of our lives; in every occasion we have, in which we may show our love to his law . . .

The world represents a rare and sumptuous palace, mankind the great family in it, and God the mighty Lord and master of it . . .

But tho' God has replenished this world with abundance of good things for man's life and comfort, yet they are all but imperfect goods. He only is the perfect good to whom they point. But alas! Men cannot see him for them; tho' they should always see him in them . . .

The world is a form; our bodies are forms; and no visible acts of devotion can be without forms. But yet the less form in religion the better, since God is a Spirit: for the more mental our worship, the more adequate to the nature of God: the more silent, the more suitable to the language of a Spirit . . .

Words are for others, not for our selves; nor for God, who hears not as bodies do; but as spirits should . . .

If we would know this dialect; we must learn of the Divine Principle in us. As we hear the dictates of that, so God hears us . . . .[14]

The first of this three volume set comes to a tender conclusion with a beautiful passage on love. The fewness and fulness of his words are striking, and the weight of his concern penetrates the heart of every person's spiritual condition:

> Love is above all; and when it prevails in us all, we shall be lovely, and in love with God and one with another.[15]

The beautiful spirit of Penn is most apparent in his words on love and death, which have not only been of comfort to thousands within the Society of Friends, but to all seekers who have sought to understand the Quaker position on life after death. He does not often rise to such spiritual heights as in the words which follow:

> The truest end of life, is to know the life that never ends.
>
> He that makes this his Care, will find it his Crown at last.
>
> And he that lives to live ever, never fears dying:
> nor can the means be terrible to him
> that heartily believes the end.
>
> For though Death be a Dark passage, it leads to Immortality,
> And that's Recompence enough for Suffering of it.
> And yet Faith lights us even through the Grave,
> being Evidence of Things not seen.
>
> And this is the Comfort of the Good,
> that the Grave cannot hold them,
> and that they live as soon as they die.
> For death is no more
> than a turning of us over from time to eternity.
>
> Death, then, being the way and condition of Life,
> we cannot love to live,
> if we cannot bear to die.
>
> They that love beyond the World, cannot be separated by it.
> Death cannot kill what never dies.
> Nor can Spirits ever be divided,
> that love and live in the same Divine Principle,
> the Root and Record of their Friendship.
> If Absence be not Death, neither is theirs.
>
> Death is but Crossing the World, as Friends do the Seas;
> they live in one another still.
> For they must needs be present,
> that love and live in that which is Omnipresent.

> In this Divine Glass, they see Face to Face;
> and their Converse is Free, as well as Pure.[16]

These words exemplify the uncontested truth that William Penn was touched by a love in which all other love is grounded. He knew that the essence of all religion was the love of God, and like most Friends of his day, he did not just talk about love, he sought to use love in the practical matters of daily life. "Let us then try what love will do," was the edict by which early Friends lived. They had witnessed the degradation of the human spirit by the use of force, and so they sought, instead, to reach people with the message of Christ by living in the spirit of love. William Penn knew the beauty of this difficult approach to human relations, and though he believed love to be the hardest lesson of the Christian faith, for this reason he was most careful to learn it.

Though *Fruits of Solitude* most assuredly belongs to the school of devotion, and was written by one who belongs to the fellowship of Christian mystics, in no way does Penn find in the scheme of existence a place for the complete withdrawal into a monastic life. This was certainly not his understanding of Christianity, nor the understanding of the other Quaker giants who are presented in this volume. He advocated, instead, a mysticism that allowed for withdrawal from the world to commune with God, and then a return to the world to carry out His will. Neither the extreme emphasis on the isolated inner life of devotion, nor the opposite extreme of constant service, marks the life of this Quaker thinker and doer. "True Godliness," writes Penn, "does not turn men out of the world but enables them to live better in it and excites their endeavor to mend it."

With this understanding of practical Christian mysticism, Penn attempts to help his children in the development of their spiritual life by writing a little volume entitled, *Fruits Of A Father's Love*. In this book his writing style differs from the abruptness in *Some* and *More Fruits Of Solitude,* taking more space for elaboration on some of the great themes of the Christian faith. Concerned about his children's "Christian and civil capacity and duty in this world," Penn begins, "My dear Children:"

> Not knowing how long it may please God to continue me amongst you, I am willing to embrace this opportunity of leaving you my advice and counsel with respect to your Christian and civil capacity and duty in this world. And I both beseech you and charge you, by the relation you have to me, and the affection I have always shown to you, and indeed received from you, that you lay up the same in your heads, with a wise and religious care.[17]

At the time of this writing William Penn was an old man for his day, fifty-six as measured by the standard of time, centuries old if judged by the more accurate standards of tireless achievement and noble suffering. As a concerned, aging parent, he wanted his children to embrace the good and avoid the evil, and he stresses the need to obey the Light of Christ, which leads persons out of the world's dark and degenerate ways to the Christian way of life. His suggestions include maintaining unity within the Society of Friends, and he shares this concern by leaving the following words:

> Above all things, my dear children, as to your communion and fellowship with Friends, be careful to keep the unity of the faith in the bond of peace . . . .[18]

These are the measured words of a disciplined member of an orderly community, anxious to preserve that which had been so dear to him throughout his life. In the span of forty-seven years he had seen this bewildered band of Christian seekers become an organized, well supported fellowship. Once they were shunned, now they were a respected community of believers. Penn had fought courageously for this new found toleration, and nothing would have pleased him more than to have had his children continue in his example, seeking unity in the bond of peace.

One of the most beautiful examples of Penn's aphormistic style is shared with his readers as he writes about the ideal of marriage, another ideal toward which he hoped his children would strive:

> Never marry but for love; but see that thou lovest what is lovely.
>
> He that minds a body and not a soul has not the better part of that relation, and will consequently want the noblest comfort of a married life.
>
> Between a man and his wife nothing ought to rule but love . . . As love ought to bring them together, so it is the best way to keep them well together.
>
> A husband and wife that love and value one another show their children and servants that they should do so too. Others visibly lose their authority in their families by their contempt of one another; and teach their children to be unnatural by their own examples.
>
> Let not enjoyment lessen, but augment, affection; it being the basest of passions to like when we have not, what we slight when we possess.
>
> Here it is we ought to search out our pleasure, where the field is large and full of variety, and of an enduring nature; sickness, poverty, or disgrace being not able to shake it, because it is not under the moving influences of worldly contingencies.
>
> Nothing can be more entire and without reserve; nothing more zealous, affectionate and sincere; nothing more contented and constant than such a couple, nor no greater temporal felicity than to be one of them.[19]

We shall better understand Penn's reason for writing *Fruits Of A Father's Love,* if we study the relationship he had with his own father. Young William did not often see his father due to Sir Admiral Penn's responsibility with the Royal Navy. Upon William Penn's conversion to Basic Christianity his father disowned him, and scorned his son's new found faith. This severed relationship between parent and child deeply affected them both, and it would seem that this little book of advice was conceived out of this sad experience. It is a volume of gentleness, born out of a lifetime of religious seeking. In it he expresses a high spiritual vision for his children, and sets before them rules of conduct, that if followed, would lead to a strong and vibrant Christian faith.

To help in the development of this experiential Christianity, Penn instructs his children on how to read the Bible, and in these few words he helps his readers to understand the Quaker belief regarding the use of Scripture:

> Having thus expressed myself to you, my dear children, as to the things of God, his truth and kingdom, I refer you to his light, grace, spirit, and truth without you, which from my youth I loved to read, and were ever blessed to me, and which I charge you to read daily; the Old Testament for history chiefly, the Psalms for meditation and devotion, the Prophets for comfort and hope, but especially the New Testament for doctrine, faith and worship; for they were given forth by holy men of God in divers ages, as they were moved by the Holy Spirit, and are the declared and revealed mind and will of the holy God to mankind under divers dispensations, and they are certainly able to make the man of God perfect, through faith unto salvation, being such a true and clear testimony to the salvation that is of God, through Christ the second Adam, the Light of the world.... I refer to you, my dear children, to the light and spirit of Jesus, that is within you, and to the Scriptures of truth without you, and such other testimonies to the one same eternal truth as have been borne in our day, and shall now descend to particulars, that you may more directly apply what I have said in general, both as to your religious and civil direction in your pilgrimage upon earth.[20]

Continuing with the concern of a Christian mystic,

Penn pours contempt on the physical things of this world and exalts the qualities of reverence and devotion:

> Beware of the pernicious lusts of the eye, and the flesh, and the pride of life... which are not of the Father, but of the world. Get higher and nobler objects for your immortal part, oh, my dear children! and be not tied to things without you... Be free; live at home — in yourselves....[21]

As he wrote these words in his seclusion, Penn no doubt had vivid memories of a confusing world that was destroying itself in hunger for things not of the spirit. "Be not tied to things without...." is a call for a separation from the externalities of the world. Penn clearly saw two realities contending for humankind — the world and the spirit. His counsel is to "... live at home — in yourselves..." and for a mystic this is an important step of development along the Christian Pathway toward the higher life in the Spirit.

In London, in May of 1712, William Penn was stricken with what his wife called "the fever," but what we today would call a stroke. This was the first of three strokes which eventually left this Quaker giant paralyzed and with little memory. After a continued and gradual worsening of health for about six years, he died on May 30, 1718, in the 74th year of his age.

William Penn has gained his own immortality by continuing to live through his writings. *Fruits Of Solitude,* being his most inspirational pieces, give witness to his life as a follower of the Light of Christ. These three volumes are a rich mine of spiritual insight, expressing Penn's religious realism and common sense. Though he was a man deeply devoted to the cause of justice, and worked for concerns which expressed man's humanity to man, he never neglected his need for spiritual nourishment, which could only come from a turning inward, an opening of his life to the refreshing springs of the Holy Spirit.

Many of the ideals for which he worked and dedicated his life have not yet been realized, and will probably not become a reality in our lifetime. However, the vision remains — the ideal is ever before us. All of life is a "Holy Experiment," lived out in worship, service, and witness, and as we seek to be followers of the Light of Christ, as William Penn sought this light, then our lives will become less dependent on our own efforts, and more dependent on the indwelling work of Christ's Spirit in our hearts.

Notes: Chapter I

[1] Catherine Owens Peare, *William Penn* (Ann Arbor: The University of Michigan Press, 1956), p. 20.
[2] Ibid. p. 40.
[3] Ibid. p. 42.
[4] William Penn, *No Cross, No Crown* (London: Society of Friends, 1930), p. 15.
[5] Ibid., p. 64.
[6] In actuality, Penn's *Fruits of Solitude* are divided into three separate volumes. *Some Fruits Of Solitude* was published in 1693, *More Fruits Of Solitude* was published in 1702, and *Fruits Of A Father's Love*, which was written shortly before 1699, was first published in 1726.
[7] Ibid., p. 10.
[8] Ibid., p. 15.
[9] William Penn, *The Rise And Progress Of The People Called Quakers* (Richmond, Indiana: Friends United Press), p. 83.
[10] Ibid., p. 64-65.
[11] William Penn, *Some Fruits Of Solitude* (London: Headley Brothers, 1905), p. 105.
[12] *Some Fruits Of Solitude;* p. 35.
[13] Ibid., p. 37.
[14] Ibid., p. 94, 96-97, 99-100, 103.
[15] Ibid., p. 110.
[16] Ibid., p. 101-102, 136-137.
[17] William Penn, *Advice of William Penn To His Children* (Philadelphia: Franklin Roberts, 1881). p. 3-4.
[18] Ibid., p. 13.
[19] *Some Fruits Of Solitude*, p. 39, 43, 44.
[20] *Fruits Of A Father's Love*, p. 14-16.
[21] Ibid., p. 23.

Chapter II

John Woolman: Apostle Of Human Freedom

"Get the writings of John Woolman by heart."
— Charles Lamb

All of the great classics of devotion discussed in this volume are inward paths to the Living Christ. In the study of their authors it is heartening to note how many are the points on which they agree, and how few the points on which they differ. These classics do not contradict one another. However they may vary in the time and style in which they were written, they are all alike in their evangelical message and sense of mystical awareness. It is of the utmost significance that these Quaker authors, drawing their inspiration obviously from a single source of Light, have based their religious life upon an identical foundation of faith, hope and love.

William Penn, John Woolman, Hannah Whitall Smith, Rufus Jones and Thomas Kelly, however separated by time and space, have arrived at the same conviction, that there is a divine purpose in life. They believe in the goodness of God and the great potential in humankind. With all of their faults, they believe that all persons carry within them the Light of Christ, and are born with the capacity to do good. It is the conviction of these authors that every living creature is a part of the whole of humankind, which has been created and directed by a purposeful God.

Within this purposeful design of God, resides the individual human soul which is embarked upon a journey, and although we are bound to come across pitfalls, we shall also discover a Living Hope. Jesus Christ is a living present reality within us throughout this life of spiritual adventure. This is the "good news" that all of the Quaker mystics extol, that, "Jesus Christ has come to teach his followers Himself!"

The all encompassing motif that binds this faith into a unit of hope is love. All of the Quaker classics of devotion agree that love unites person to person, and person with God. In the words of John Woolman, "Love was the first motion," and he, like the others, was a great lover who believed with the sensitivity and open faith of a child.

The character of John Woolman, like that of Christ his Master, was essentially simple. This simplicity, however, was not that of a sterile uniformity, for at the core of this New Jersey rustic there was a constant perplexity. He was torn between the life of Christian contemplation and the duties of the active life. He was never able to resolve this contradiction, and by keeping the two in constant tension his character was more fully developed. Since the truly religious man or woman is one who is always seeking a balance of prayer and service, rival claims upon our life from the world within and the world without will always be with us. We can be heartened by the knowledge that John Woolman lived in this antithesis, and felt the tensions between the demands of prayer and service. He was unable to live in both worlds at once, yet he was able to maintain a balance.

John Woolman knew by nature what many of us have to learn, that in the Christian faith a sense of reality is preserved only so long as there is a connection between word and deed. One reason why *The Journal of John Woolman* is a classic in religious literature, is because it shows how Woolman was able to translate religious conviction into actions. The distinction between the life of devotion and the life of service is not denied, but the former is forever in the process of passing into the later. This connection, which Woolman has so effectively exemplified, has been an important reason why he is a model of Christian conduct, not only in the Society of Friends, but throughout the Christian community.

In the biographical note preceding *The Journal Of John Woolman* in the Harvard Classics, Charles W. Eliot writes: "His own words in this *Journal* of an extraordinary simplicity and charm, are the best expressions of a personality which in its ardor, purity of motive, breadth of sympathy, and clear spiritual insight, gives Woolman a place among the uncanonized saints of America." As one reads John Woolman's *Journal*, he finds that President Eliot has not been too generous with his praise. It is truly a masterpiece of American literature, and portrays a man who was able to combine a disciplined inner life with God and a deep concern for social justice amongst his fellowmen.

The study of John Woolman is important to all Christians who are seeking a model by which to live. He combined in his life the elements of *Simplicity* in living style, *Sensitivity* to the concerns of others, *Toughness* when confronting social injustice, and *Faithfulness* in his life of worship. He lived a balanced life, always seeking the guidance of the Inward Teacher before setting out on a journey of social concern. He never rushed into important decisions, but waited until he felt the power of Christ's presence with him before proceeding. He was a man acquainted with despair and grief, yet he was able to see through these times of agony because his faith rested on a Perfect Love, which no human situation could destroy. This was the same sustaining Love that strengthened the early Friends as they struggled for religious freedom in England —

hundreds of whom died in prison, and it was the same Spirit of Love that sustained the courageous Quaker pioneers as they traveled the Atlantic Ocean to settle in the Colony of Pennsylvania. The experience of the Quaker fellowship of suffering was Woolman's experience, and he learned early, regardless of situation, to seek the leading of the Divine Presence, the giver and sustainer of life.

John Woolman was born in 1720, in a little village called Burlington in the Colony of New Jersey. His grandfather, John, had settled in this colony 42 years earlier to escape religious persecution. This section of New Jersey was made up almost entirely of English Quakers who had sought refuge from the tyranny of English rule. John Woolman's father, Samuel, was a fruit grower and a farmer, and when young John was not studying the great books at his disposal, he was helping his father on the farm. The formal education Woolman received was in the village school, which began at the age of four, and lasted for only ten years. However, receiving the encouragement he needed at home, he continued a life-long course of self-education, reading constantly, saturating himself in the Bible, the classics of the Quaker faith by William Penn and Robert Barclay, and devotional literature, such as *The Imitation of Christ* by Thomas a Kempis. With this rich background of study, we can discern how Woolman was able to write so beautifully and touch our hearts so significantly. His teachers were the masters of Christian devotion.

Woolman begins his *Journal** with a description of his early years, which were a cycle of seeking after God, developing a keen sense of His presence, on occasion falling from this presence, and then seeking reconciliation. An early account in the *Journal* depicts the frivolous and the serious conscientious side of young

---

*Throughout this chapter I shall be using the Phillips P. Moulton edition of the *Journal*.

Woolman. This tender scene has been memorialized in a beautiful stained-glass window in Plymouth Congregational Church, Minneapolis, Minnesota, and is the only window ever done in memory of a Quaker. The moving account shares how young John was on his way to a neighbor's house when he saw a robin sitting on her nest, and as he approached, the robin flew about chirping, obviously expressing concern for her babies. Without thinking, Woolman began to throw stones at her until one hit her, and she fell dead. At first this exploit made him proud, but upon considering more carefully what he had done, Woolman was stricken with horror. The words which follow are his, and they depict, in a touching way, the gentleness of this Quaker saint:

> I beheld her lying dead and thought those young ones for which she was so careful must now perish for want of their dam to nourish them; and after some painful consideration on the subject, I climbed up the tree, took all the young birds and killed them, supposing that better than to leave them to pine away and die miserably, and believed in this case that Scripture proverb was fulfilled, "The tender mercies of the wicked are cruel" (Prov. 12:10). I then went on my errand, but for some hours could think of little else but the cruelties I had committed, and was much troubled.[1]

The Eighteenth Century John Woolman was very much like the Thirteenth Century Francis Of Assisi, since both had an instinctive identity with nature, an identification which is very different from the dualism with which the modern person is familiar. In recent decades we have developed an "Us vs. The Rest Of Nature" mentality. The swallows to whom Francis Of Assisi preached, and the robins about whom John Woolman was so disturbed, seem not to be a part of our Christian concern. Our humanistic age seems to have all but destroyed nature mysticism.

The story of John Woolman's early years is the story

of conflict. Throughout his adolescence he was attracted to youthful vanities which separated him from his righteous Christian fellowship, and though his youth does not seem to be much different from any other young person's growing years, upon reflection the sensitive Woolman was appalled at his own wantonness:

> While I meditate on the gulf toward which I traveled and reflect on my youthful disobedience, for these things I weep; mine eye runneth down with water.[2]

His youthful exploits were finally overcome, and by looking seriously at the means by which he was drawn from Christ and "His Way Of Life," Woolman was led to see how the cravings of sense must be governed by a divine principle. In his times of "waiting upon the Lord," Woolman felt the power of Christ surround his life and provide the strength he needed to overcome selfish desires. His struggle was not over, but he was now able to face life with an assuredness that would help keep him on the path of Christian obedience.

Such a change in his lifestyle was shocking. The liberating power of Christ that released Woolman from the shackles of former vanities was difficult for him to explain, and he tells his readers:

> While I silently ponder on that change wrought in me, I find no language equal to it nor any means to convey to another a clear idea of it. I looked upon the works of God in this visible creation and an awfulness covered me; my heart was tender and often contrite, and a universal love to my fellow creatures increased in me. This will be understood by such who have trodden in the same path. Some glances of real beauty may be seen in their faces who dwell in true meekness. There is a harmony in the sound of that voice to which divine love gives utterance, and some appearance of right order in their temper and conduct whose passions are fully regulated. Yet all these do not fully show forth that inward life to such who have felt it, but this white stone and new name is known

rightly to such only who have it.[3]

At the age of 21, John Woolman was asked by a businessman in Mt. Holly if he would tend his shop and keep his books. Following a discussion of this proposal with his father, they both agreed that he should accept the position. At this point in his life, students of the *Journal* can clearly discern an important change in Woolman's character. Having left his former wanton ways, he began a new life inwardly, and he also started a new life outwardly, entering the world of business, and making a new home in Mt. Holly. Not only does he change his physical surroundings, but he has changed his attitude about life as well. Continuing from this point the Woolman depicted in the *Journal* is a man sure of himself and positive about the direction his life should take. No longer do we see a young man confused about his relationship with God, living from one youthful vanity to the next, for now he is confident in himself, and with the guiding hand of God he is able to turn away from the friends with whom he engaged in frivolous behavior. The religious vocation which was so long developing in his youth has now come into maturity, and though Woolman never quits growing spiritually, at this point in his life he finds the "life in the Spirit" which he has so long been seeking. Developing this new life, becoming sensitive to the leadings of the Christ within, now becomes the "magnificent obsession" of Woolman's being.

From beginning to end, *The Journal of John Woolman* is lighted with a moral perception which is very touching. He understood, as few persons have understood, how difficult and complex are the problems of the human conscience. This aspect of Woolman's character was matured in his slow and agonizing struggle over the issue of human slavery, and at the close of the first chapter of the Moulton edition of the *Journal,* Woolman shares his first confrontation between his conscience and this increasingly apparent social evil:

> My employer, having a Negro woman, sold her and directed me to write a bill of sale, the man being waiting who bought her. The thing was sudden, and though the thoughts of writing an instrument of slavery for one of my fellow creatures felt uneasy, yet I remembered I was hired by the year, that it was my master who directed me to do it, and that it was an elderly man, a member of our Society, who bought her; so through weakness I gave way and wrote it, but at executing it, I was so afflicted in my mind that I said before my master and the Friend that I believed slavekeeping to be a practice inconsistent with the Christian religion. This in some degree abated my uneasiness, yet as often as I reflected seriously upon it I thought I should have been clearer if I had desired to be excused from it as a thing against my conscience, for such it was.[4]

This experience was the beginning of a 29 year crusade against slavery, which lasted until his death. While others during this period of American history accepted slavery uncritically, Woolman was repulsed by the sin which allowed one color of human being to enslave another. It was truly contradictory to the teachings of Christ, and Woolman could not stand inconsistency in moral behavior.

Like all of the Quaker mystics here discussed, the seed of Christ in John Woolman was nurtured and developed within the community of the Religious Society of Friends. John Woolman was a great individual, but he was great because he realized that he belonged to, and was supported by a fellowship that reached beyond the confines of the self. He understood that it is only in the Christian community that individuals can fully realize their potential for spiritual development. The Light of Christ within each person grows as he shares in a corporate setting with like-minded believers, and though the times of solitude when seekers reach God directly during periods of personal worship are very important, they must always remember that this is only a part of the total worship experience. Without the corporate expression, the Seed eventually withers and dies. Without the support and fellowship which can come from genuine Christian community, the individual follower of Christ is cut-off from the uplifting support of love, care, and concern which is needed in the life of ministry and service to the world. John Woolman spent many hours alone in prayer, and discovered early in his experience that prayer is foundational in a life of ministry. The life of inner devotion strengthened Woolman for a life of outer service, but never was this life of prayer and ministry seen as a totally individualistic undertaking. Always he sought the strength and support of his Religious Society, and he received it, thus enabling him to be such an effective Friends' minister.

Woolman's *Journal* is filled with "conditional" leadings. Before each of his many visits to Friends around America and England, he sought the support and approval of his Meeting. "... after a conference with some elderly Friends I agreed to go...."[5] "... and with the unity of Friends, we traveled about two weeks visiting Friends...."[6] "Feeling an exercise in relation to a visit to the southern parts to increase upon me, I acquainted our Monthly Meeting therewith and obtained their certificate."[7] Always Woolman took his concern to his Meeting for their approval before proceeding in his ministerial tasks. In the Friends Community, Woolman found his base for operation. D. Elton Trueblood writes on this important aspect of Woolman's life:

> The superiority of Woolman rests squarely on a Quaker base. Though he was clearly superior to the surrounding Quakers, his excellence is unthinkable apart from the Quaker cultural setting. He was extremely different from the stormy George Fox or

from the courtly atmosphere which men like Fox and Penn made possible. Woolman was a universal Saint,

> as so many kinds of people have been quick to recognize, but this saintliness was Quaker before it was universal.[8]

John Woolman's ministry and life style were nurtured in the Christian fellowship of the Society of Friends. Not all Quakers are or were like Woolman, but in him one can see the possibility of the Quaker potential. By studying his life and his writings we learn about the Quaker ideal, for he provides us with the best single introduction to what Quakers seek to contribute to the world. This contribution is a combination of boldness in the face of social evil, and sensitive tenderness in dealing with those who are the oppressors. This paradox of Quakerism is also the paradox of Woolman, and when we study his individual qualities, we arrive at glimpses of the truth which mere doctrine can never provide.

Feeling the burdens of business increasing upon him, Woolman felt led to devote more time to his main vocation — the Christian ministry. He decided that the best way to gain more independence was to become a tailor, since in this way he could make a living without the responsibility of big business. As his tailoring practice grew, however, he found it becoming burdensome, and so he sent many of his customers to competitors. He might have been a rich and successful merchant, but the glories of wealth did not interest him, since he feared the entanglement of material things which hindered growth in the spiritual life. He would rather do without certain luxuries so that he could be a more effective minister for Jesus Christ.

In his liberation from the snarls of business, Woolman found more time to be a traveling minister, and in 1746 he obtained his Meeting's permission to travel with a companion through Virginia and into North Carolina — the heart of slave country. On this mission he saw, in a vivid way, the evils of slavery, and felt uneasy staying with people who were living off the hard labor of these captive human beings. The following words are one of Woolman's best known sayings about the menace of slavery to the future of America, which was inspired by his absolute certainty that there is an objective moral design in our world, and for our own good we best follow it:

> I saw in these southern provinces so many vices and corruptions increased by this trade and this way of life that it appeared to me as a dark gloominess hanging over the land; and though now many willingly run into it, yet in future the consequence will be grievous to posterity! I express it as it hath appeared to me, not at once nor twice, but as a matter fixed on my mind.[9]

He returned home following his southern experience, convinced more than ever that slavery was an evil that must be vanquished. The inside changes that began to work in Woolman following this mission had their roots in the Friends' belief of equality for all, which developed from the Quaker understanding of the Light of Christ within every person. He was ready to be the voice of a new order that had no place for the enslavement of fellow human beings. He alone carried the burden of convincing his own Religious Society of the need to be done with this unchristian practice, which in turn carried the burden of trying to change the attitude of America.

Out of the silent working of Woolman's inner life, came a strength which enabled him to endure harsh criticism and constant frustration. In the anti-slavery messages that he would deliver, there would be reason and passion arising out of them that silenced his most vocal critics. Since he was well aware of the risks of self-display which the prophet is liable, he knew, if others did not, that he was in the toils of something greater than self-agrandizement. He was pleading for the recovery of our lost humanity.

After an absence of ten years, Woolman once again felt the Lord leading him to visit the south. While there he heard many defenses of slavery, the most common being that since the black people lived in such wretched conditions in Africa, it was a kindness to bring them to America. John Woolman cut through this self-deception like a knife, responding in the following firm and clear way:

> ... If compassion on the Africans in regard to their domestic troubles were the real motives of our purchasing them, that spirit of tenderness being attended to would incite us to use them kindly, that as strangers brought out of affliction their lives might be happy among us; and as they are human creatures, whose souls are as precious as ours and who may receive the same help and comfort of the Holy Scriptures as we do, we could not omit suitable endeavors to instruct them therein. But while we manifest by our conduct that our views in purchasing them are to advance ourselves, and while our buying captives taken in war animates those parties to push on that war and increase desolations amongst them, to say they live unhappy in Africa is far from being an argument in our favour.[10]

And then, in one of the most prophetic insights ever expounded, Woolman relates his convictions concerning the logical outcome of this gross injustice:

> ... The present circumstances of these provinces to me appears difficult, that the slaves look like a burdensome stone to such who burden themselves with them, and that if the white people retain a resolution to prefer their outward prospects of gain to all other considerations and do not act conscientiously toward them as fellow creatures, I believe that burden will grow heavier till times change in a way disagreeable to us ...[11]

These words were spoken 104 years before the attack on Fort Sumter.

John Woolman was truest to his genius and his vocation when he undertook a journey into Indian territory to try and help resolve the differences between the Indians and the white settlers. As he traveled deeper into the frontier of Western Pennsylvania, he meditated upon the circumstances of the Native Americans and how they had been driven from their homeland by the superior force of the English. In this lonely journey he was deeply bothered by the spreading of a wrong spirit that led to the fighting, and he saw, at this early date, how the seeds were being sown for much greater conflict as the white settlers moved westward.

While traveling on this important mission, Woolman felt led to think on the progression of events leading him to take such a momentous journey. In these words we learn the basis upon which all else followed, not only for this journey, but for all of the concerns that Woolman had championed:

> *Love was the first motion*, and then a concern arose to spend some time with the Indians, that I might feel and understand their life and the Spirit they live in, if haply I might receive some instruction from them, or they be in any degree helped forward by my following the leadings of Truth amongst them.[12]

After a week of travel through the wilderness, Woolman and his traveling companions reached the Indian village of Wyalusing. His visit was brief, culminating in a Meeting for Worship with the Indians. After words were exchanged through interpreters, Woolman felt led to pray without the use of interpretation, and following what must have been a most reverent confession to God, Papunchang, Chief of this Indian village, expressed to an interpreter what is now a famous saying among Quakers: "I love to feel where words come from."[13] John Woolman and Papunchang had made contact through Divine mediation.

The earthly pilgrimage of John Woolman ended while

visiting Friends in England, hoping to press upon the members of London Yearly Meeting the cause of the black race. Although he was weak, the Spirit of the Lord was upon him, leading him to make a witness among the Friends living where Quakerism had its beginning. He took passage on the ship called *Mary and Elizabeth*, and chose to travel across the Atlantic by steerage instead of cabin. His reason for subjecting himself to this discomfort was a social testimony against class distinction, and when questioned by the owner of the ship about his decision, Woolman explained:

> ... I told the owner that I had at several times in my travels seen great oppressions on this continent, at which my heart had been much affected and brought often into a feeling of the state of the sufferers ... And having many times engaged, in the fear and love of God, to labour with those under whom the oppressed have been borne down and afflicted, I have often perceived that a view to get riches and provide estates for children, to live comfortable to customs which stand in that spirit wherein men have regard to the honours of this world — that in pursuit of these things I had seen many entangled in the spirit of oppression, and the exercise of my soul been such that I could not find peace in joying in anything which I saw was against that wisdom which is pure.[14]

After six weeks in the steerage of the *Mary and Elizabeth*, Woolman arrived in London. The London Yearly Meeting of the Religious Society of Friends was then in session, and not wanting to take time to bathe and change clothes, he made his way directly to Devonshire House where the Yearly Meeting of 1772 was being held. One can imagine the stares he received from the distinguished English Quakers when he arrived at the meeting house, dressed in undyed clothing, and showing a great deal of wear after riding in the steerage of a ship for several weeks. The cultivated Friends of England thought that they had a crank on their hands, and so their first concern when he arrived was to try and get rid of him. One Friend arose in meeting and spoke, suggesting that Woolman might now consider his mission accomplished so that he could feel free to go home. The sensitive Woolman was deeply hurt, and sat in meeting weeping openly.

After sitting for a long period of time, his weeping ended, Woolman stood and said that he did not yet feel released from his ministerial visit to England, but that he knew he could not travel without their permission. Therefore, he would stay, but with no expense to English Friends. He said he could employ his trade, if the Quakers in England would hire him. He sat down, and in the encompassing silence which followed Woolman again arose, and this time he was able to convince all present that he truly had a ministry to share. When he sat down, even the Friend who suggested that he return home to America confessed that he was in error, and expressed his support to Woolman, asking him to remain in England as long as he felt led to stay.

Soon after Yearly Meeting, the man from the Colony of New Jersey started north. He was anxious to see the country where Fox and the "First Publishers of Truth" began their ministry, but he proceeded on foot, refusing to ride in the stagecoaches because of the harsh treatment the drivers and horses received. Upon arriving in York, Woolman went to the home of Thomas Priestman, where he stayed while ministering to the people of this great Cathedral City. Soon after his arrival, however, he showed symptoms of small pox, the disease which he most dreaded. The Quakers of York came to his aid, and worked vigorously trying to nurse him back to health, but soon he was dead. John Woolman left this earthly life on October 7, 1772.

The Society of Friends has been given a rich heritage. She is the community of Christians out of which her sons and daughters have recorded their spiritual experiences in the pages of confession and self-analysis, which offer to us, her students, an endless field of illustrations from which to learn. But it was left to a man who won his lonely way from darkness to light to share with us, in a practical way, as no spiritual recluse could ever speak. The testimony of our own experience validates the practical message of John Woolman, since we all know the struggles of youth and the easy temptations that obstruct our paths. We can all feel with Woolman as he is forced to choose between loyalty to his employer or his conscience, as he writes a bill of sale for a slave. The circumstances are not the same, but the feelings he shares with us are unmistakably our feelings, experienced in countless tasks throughout our own lives. In reading *The Journal of John Woolman*, all that is within us acknowledges the truth of his interpretations of conscientious responsibility. We not only hail him as a master of words, seer of visions and a sensitive in the realm of the spirit, but we know him as one who attained a level of spirituality for which we all long. We see him as one who was able to move from his conscientious intentions, to concrete actions, in a way which was consistent.

The striking features of Woolman's character were Christian simplicity and meekness, united with an ardent love for his fellow creatures. His simple ways and hard toil, along with a deep reverence for Christ, make him one of the world's rare practical Christian mystics. This simple man from New Jersey sought radical reforms in society, calling for an end to slavery 100 years before the outbreak of the Civil War. He refused to wear dyed clothing because of the conditions under which those who made the dye were forced to work. His life was in unity with the suffering of the American Indians as they were lied to and cheated out of their land. Everywhere and at all times John Woolman sought justice for the oppressed and refused to be part of a system that destroyed persons for the sake of material gain. Coupled with these deep social concerns was a strong Christian faith that upheld him during the most difficult times, and out of which his concerns arose. From boyhood Woolman learned that he was surrounded with a sense of God's goodness and nearness, and he learned early in life about the strength and sense of purpose which one can receive through prayer. In times of distress he could always find help from his ever present companion, the Living Christ.

The Journal of John Woolman is a simple record of his traveling ministry and his ever deepening interior life. In the *Lectures* on the *Harvard Classics,* William Roscoe Thayer testifies to the spiritual nature of Woolman's *Journal* by calling it, "the austerely sincere record of a soul that does not spend its time in casuistical interpretations of the quibbles propounded by medieval theologians, but *dwells consciously in the immediate presence of the Living God."* (Italics mine) Through this masterpiece of literature we know Woolman as one who sought, struggled, and attained a life of holy obedience. For him, "love was the first motion," and as we seek to live our lives in the Light of Christ, we discover that love is contagious. As we enter into a deeper, more full relationship with Him, we discover, as John Woolman discovered, that "Our Gracious Creator cares and provides for all his Creatures. His tender mercies are over all his works; and, so far as his love influences our minds, so far we become interested in his workmanship, and feel a desire to take hold of every opportunity to lessen the distresses of the afflicted and increase the happiness of the Creation. Here we have a prospect of one common interest, from which our own is inseparable, that to turn all the treasures we possess into the channel of Universal Love becomes the business of our lives."[15]

Notes: Chapter II

[1] Phillips P. Moulton edition, *The Journal and Major Essays of John Woolman* (New York: Oxford University Press, 1971), p. 24-25.
[2] Ibid., p. 25.
[3] Ibid., p. 29.
[4] Ibid., p. 32-33.
[5] Ibid., p. 34.
[6] Ibid., p. 45.
[7] Ibid., p. 58.
[8] D. Elton Trueblood, *The People Called Quakers* (New York: Harper and Row, 1966). p. 152-153.
[9] *The Journal and Major Essays of John Woolman*, p. 38.
[10] Ibid., p. 62.
[11] Ibid., p. 62.
[12] Ibid., p. 127.
[13] Ibid., p. 133.
[14] Ibid., p. 164-165.
[15] Ibid., p. 241.

Chapter III

Hannah Whitall Smith: Teacher of The Interior Life

"... *she is a fascinating woman, incapable, it seems, of writing a dull word.*"

— Jessamyn West

Few persons realize the close connection between the militant atheist philosopher, Bertrand Russell, and the gentle Quaker evangelist, Hannah Whitall Smith. This is not a connection in terms of thought, for no two persons could have agreed less philosophically, but, instead, a familial relationship with resulted when Russell married Alys, Mrs. Smith's daughter, thus becoming her son-in-law. As an avowed atheist, Russell totally rejected the kind of Christian belief for which his mother-in-law stood. In the chapter, "A Free Man's Worship," which appears in his volume, *Mysticism and Logic*, Bertrand Russell eloquently stated his unbelief, avowing the ultimate meaninglessness of human life:

> ... Man is the product of causes which had no prevision of the end they were achieving ... his origin, his growth, his hopes and fears, his loves and his beliefs, are but the outcome of accidental callocations of atoms ... No fire, no heroism, no intensity of thought and feeling, can preserve an individual life beyond the grave ... all the labours of the ages, all the noonday brightness of human genius, are destined to extinction in the vast death of the solar system, and ... the whole temple of man's achieve-

ment must inevitably be buried beneath the debris of a Universe in ruins — all these things, if not quite beyond dispute, are yet so nearly certain, that no philosophy which rejects them can hope to stand . . .[1]

In this same articulate literary style that made Russell famous, he closes this chapter in the following words:

> Brief and powerless is man's life; on him and all his race the slow, sure doom falls pitiless and dark. Blind to good and evil, reckless of destruction, omnipotent matter rolls on its relentless way . . .[2]

These are eloquent words, and the serious reader must conclude that if God is not, then Russell is right. Not to believe in an omnipotent God must inevitably bring one to the same philosophical conclusion to which Russell was brought. But, if God is, then our philosophy of life must include an element of hope, which is non-existent in an atheistic view of the world.

A few years before these words were penned by Bertrand Russell, Hannah Whitall Smith, his Quaker mother-in-law, wrote the following letter to her son, Logan Pearsall Smith:

> I do not preach much, as I am sure thee will give me credit for, but I just want to say that but for my unswerving faith in a God of love and wisdom, and my absolute certainty that He cares for me and mine, I should have been crushed with despair long ago. Life has not contained much trouble for thee yet, darling Son, but when it comes, remember that thy mother has assured thee that there is comfort and peace in the grand fact that God IS.[3]

The inequality of life is nowhere more clearly seen than in the thinking of these two persons. Living in the same world, at the same time, even in the same family, Hannah Whitall Smith concluded that "God IS," and Bertrand Russell concluded that "God IS NOT." In the classic of Quaker devotion discussed in this chapter, the reader discovers the depth of faith with which Mrs. Smith reaches her unshakeable conclusion.

Over one-hundred years have passed since *The Christian's Secret Of A Happy Life* was first published. The fame of Hannah Whitall Smith and her joyous little classic of religious literature is widespread, and still growing today. She was a Quaker optimist who found a beauty and goodness in life during a time when humanity was shrouded in a blanket of negativism. Her manner and style have endeared her to countless persons seeking a God of love and a meaningful purpose for humankind.

Her writing is well known to those who are in the advanced stages of the Spiritual Higher Life, yet it has also come into the possession of thousands in the world who are new to the life of contemplation and Christian service, offering assurance, hope, and strength. Devoting herself, as she did, to being a teacher in the interior life, she succeeded so well that she is respected and loved as a gifted instructor, who did more in her generation than any other to lead people to Christ, and to what she calls the "Abundant Life." To Hannah Whitall Smith it was given to speak to the world, in her holy optimism and plain speech, the Good News of Jesus Christ. She was not a scholarly theologian using confusing terms, since this was not her purpose. She revealed her "secret," instead, through illustrations of common life, and wrote in simple understandable language.

Hannah Whitall Smith belongs to the inner circle of Quaker mystics who have had a sure grasp of many of the central truths of spiritual religion. She dedicated her life to expounding these invisible truths as she understood them through God's word revelation and transforming presence. She understood her mission as bearing witness to the Light of Christ within the soul, and bringing seekers into the fellowship of the Spirit of God. Hers was not a denominational proselytism, but a universal mission devoted to renewing the individual, and therefore the Christian church.

No Christian mystical writer before her, or after, has described the steps toward attainment of the Higher Life in a way so natural and so clearly within reach of all. Her gifts were unique, and as a Quaker woman she was allowed to fully develop them. The Society of Friends recognized at their inception the equality of the sexes, and encouraged the ministry of women. The words of the Apostle Paul were inspirational to this liberal understanding:

> For as many of you as were baptized into Christ have put on Christ. There is neither Jew nor Greek, *there is neither male nor female;* for you are *all one in Christ Jesus.* (Gal. 3:27-28 RSV.)

As the students of Hannah Whitall Smith, we can be grateful for the freedom she was given to share her God-given talent for writing. She was a born writer, and not to have been allowed to express this gift because of her sex would have been a sin.

The author of *The Christian's Secret Of A Happy Life* can best be studied by reviewing her life in terms of epochs. In her spiritual autobiography *The Unselfishness Of God*, she tells about the development of her interior life through four different stages, which I shall label as follows: 1) The period of "morbid self-introspection," 2) The period of assurance, 3) The period of discovery, and 4) The period of the "higher life." It was out of this fourth period that she produced the devotional classic, *The Christian's Secret Of A Happy Life*.

H.W.S. (the pen-name of Hannah Whitall Smith) was born in Philadelphia, on February 7, 1832. Her childhood was a happy one, since it was the belief of her father that everyone would mature in a better way if they had "a happy childhood tucked under their jackets." At the age of sixteen she had what can be called a mystical experience, which she came to regard as a time of "morbid self-introspection." This time of introspection lasted until her marriage to Robert Pearsall Smith, a fellow Quaker and glass manufacturer of Philadelphia. During her first few years of marriage she had serious inward spiritual struggles. It was during this same period that a daughter Nelly, and a son Frank were born. Nelly died at the age of five and Frank at the age of eighteen. The death of her daughter came at a particularly vulnerable time for H.W.S., and was the culmination of a religious struggle which led to her conversion. At this point she enters the period of assurance, and is released from her self-examination. Shortly thereafter, however, she had a very important revelation, which she described as the discovery of the "unselfishness of God." This revelation matured her in the life of the Spirit, and she entered the third period, the epoch of *discovery*.

In 1865, H.W.S. had to uproot her family from Germantown, Pennsylvania, and move to Millville, New Jersey where her husband was transferred because of his work. Being cut off from her former friends and associates, Mrs. Smith went through a period of depression which brought her to the final stage in her earthly religious development. This fourth epoch can be called the period of the "higher life," in which she consecrated her entire being to the Will of God. In the classic of devotion here discussed, we discover the secret of this "higher life," or the "life hid with Christ in God."

Hannah Whitall Smith had a deep love for children, and it was this maternal aspect of marriage which she most cherished. As mentioned earlier, two of her children died young, but three survived to adulthood. Mary was born in 1864 and Logan and Alys were born during the years at Millville. Logan Pearsall Smith grew up to be a gifted writer, his most impressive works being *Unforgotten Years,* which is his autobiography, and *A Religious Rebel,* which is a collection of letters written by his mother and edited by him. In *Unforgotten Years*, Logan Smith has shared some valuable recollections about his mother, and he relates one of the most dramatic confrontations of her ministry by telling what happened when she and her family arrived in England for their first ministerial visit. Almost immediately after setting foot on the English shore, the Smiths were escorted by some leading evangelicals of England to a drawing room where a meeting was summoned to determine whether their doctrine was sound, according to the strictest standards. The meeting went well except for one point, and it became the major concern of those gathered. From something Hannah Whitall Smith had written or said, these strict Christians were unsure of her position on the doctrine of Eternal Torment.

Mrs. Smith believed in Hell, but the point of contention was whether she believed that its torments were destined to endure forever. In fact, she did not, and although her husband and close associates sought to change her mind, when the crisis came and the question was plainly stated, she said truthfully and with no reservations that she did not. Logan Pearsall Smith writes on what happened at this point:

> She knew that her own and perhaps her husband's career as expositors of the Gospel might be ruined by this avowal; she had agreed that it would be wiser to give evasive answers on this point; but she suddenly felt that if she was questioned she must say what she thought, whatever might be the consequences; and if she had been capable of using such a profane expression she would have told herself that she didn't care a damn.
>
> She could not, she avowed to the assembled company, believe that the God she worshipped as a God of love was capable of such awful cruelty; sinners, of course, He punished, but that He had decreed that their torments should be unending was to her a horrible belief.

> Her auditors were inexpressibly dismayed by this declaration; the myrtle, in Keat's phrase, 'sickened in a thousand wreaths;' the company was on the point of breaking up in confusion when from the depths of that great drawing-room there floated forward, swathed in rich Victorian draperies and laces, a tall and stately lady, who kissed my mother, and said, 'My dear, I don't believe it either.'
>
> This dramatic moment was, perhaps, a turning point in my life, since, if it had not occurred, our family would no doubt have soon returned to America, and the ties and friendships which drew us all back again to England would never have been formed. For this lady who thus intervened and took my mother under her protection was, as it were, the queen of evangelical Christians; and her acceptance, afterwards confirmed by that of her husband, William Cowper Temple, silenced all opposition and no further objections were suggested.[4]

Mrs. Temple became Hannah Whitall Smith's closest friend while in England. She was a beautiful saintly woman, in whose character Mrs. Smith could find but one flaw. Lady Mount Temple could never grasp the difference between right and wrong, where no cruelty was involved. The Teacher of the Interior Life would try to explain to her the distinction in morals, and Lady Temple would say she understood, but before long they soon left her mind. Again, Logan Smith shares an example of the kind of interaction that took place between his mother and her best friend:

> When Oscar Wilde was out on bail between his two trials, she (Mrs. Temple) wrote him a friendly letter, inviting him to pay her a visit, by which letter, Oscar Wilde tells us, he was greatly touched. Her family, the Tollemaches, were a wild family, much given to misbehavior, and when one or another got in disgrace she would invite the offender to her home and would often send for my mother, as one familiar with right

and wrong, to come and help the erring one back to the righteous path. I remember my mother's telling of one occasion when a Tollemache, married to a foreign prince, had run away from him with a lover, and then had been placed under Lady Mount Temple's roof to be made to realize the impropriety of her conduct. My mother was as usual summoned, and arrived in her Quaker garb and with her Bible, to help in this work of moral reformation. The Bible was read, there were prayers and exhortations, and all seemed to be going on in a most satisfactory manner, till one day, entering the old lady's writing room, my mother noticed that she was trying to conceal a piece of paper, and, when questioned, she confessed that she was composing a telegram for the lover of the erring lady to come and join them, since, as she put it, she felt that Matilda was feeling so lonely without him.[5]

In *Unforgotten Years* Logan Smith also tells of the close association between his family and Walt Whitman, who was a frequent guest in their home. He writes about Whitman's "genial presence" and his quiet departures in this way:

> He became indeed a familiar and friendly inmate of the house, whose genial presence, even when we did not see him could hardly pass unnoticed, for he had the habit of singing 'Old Jim Crow' when not occupied in conversation, and his loud and cheerful voice could be heard echoing every morning from the bathroom or the water closet. His arrivals were always unannounced; he would appear when he liked, stay as long as he liked; and then one morning we would find at breakfast a penciled note to say that he had departed early, having had for the present enough of our society.[6]

This experience in the Smith home was not the first time the great poet had had contact with Quakers, since as a small boy Walt Whitman was greatly influenced by Elias Hicks. He did not know this formative Quaker figure personally, but he was held in such high esteem by

Whitman's parents that this reverence made the sensitive boy more receptive to the kind of liberal thinking Hicks preached. Elton Trueblood writes the following in his essay on Whitman entitled, "The Fullness of The God-Head Dwelt In Every Blade of Grass," which is found in Jessamyn West's *The Quaker Reader:*

> The evidence that the mood of Hicks was contagious is found . . . in the similarity of the dominant message of Walt Whitman and the dominant message of Elias Hicks . . . 'Always,' says Whitman, 'Elias Hicks gives the service of pointing to the fountain of all naked theology, all religion, all worship, all the truth to which you are possibly eligible — namely in yourself and your inherent relations. Others talk of Bibles, saints, churches, exhortation, vicarious atonements — the canons outside of yourself and apart from man . . . .[7]

The poetry of Whitman clearly shows how contagious Elias Hicks was, and brings to mind the question asked by Elton Trueblood, "Was it an accident that one Long Islander loved to say that the fullness of the godhead dwelt in every blade of grass, and another Long Islander called his poems *Leaves Of Grass?*"[8]

In his old age Walt Whitman wrote a eulogy of this aged Quaker, and was, perhaps, written in the Smith home during one of his many visits. Had Hannah Whitall Smith known of this she would have been shocked, for in the evangelical circles she frequented, the name of Hicks was ranked along with cursing. Already neighbors and relatives considered Whitman a corrupting influence, and as a result of his publication, *Leaves Of Grass,* the children of these relatives and neighbors were forbidden to visit the Smith home when the poet was known to be in residence.

Hannah Whitall Smith, like John Woolman and William Penn before her, was a practical Christian mystic. She never allowed her faith to be severed from the realities of daily living. She was a fervent reformer, working hard for temperance, world peace, and the broadening influence of women in society. She lived to be seventy-nine, which was long enough to enjoy many fun times with her grandchildren, and we find a delightful account of these later years given by her granddaughter Ray Strachey in her book, *A Quaker Grandmother.*

In many ways the Philadelphia Quaker woman was a forerunner of Thomas Kelly, sharing many years earlier much of what Kelly said in his essay on *Holy Obedience.* At points she is archaic in her language, but the essential message of the genuineness of God's guidance is timeless, regardless of writing style. The radiant joy of Hannah Whitall Smith is evident on every page of this reflection from the Light of Christ. She writes as one who discovered the Truth about life, and she seeks to share her discovery with all who will take time to read her modestly written, yet deeply moving masterpiece of literature. Since it is not written primarily for the aesthetic or spiritual genius, but for the common man and woman who seek God in the routine duties of daily living, the secret she unlocks is shared in easy to understand illustrations. In a confrontation which changed her life, H.W.S. was given insight into the true meaning of what the religion of Christ ought to be. She writes:

> A keen observer once said to me, "You Christians seem to have a religion that makes you miserable. You are like a man with a headache. He does not want to get rid of his head, but it hurts him to keep it. You cannot expect outsiders to seek very earnestly for anything so uncomfortable." Then for the first time I saw, as in a flash, that the religion of Christ ought to be, and was meant to be, to its possessors, not something to make them miserable, but something to make them happy; and I began then and there to ask the Lord to show me the secret of a happy Christian life.[9]

In these words from page one of her book, Hannah Whitall Smith presents her basic purpose for writing. *The Christian's Secret Of A Happy Life* is full of feeling, yet it is not a book on the religious emotions; it is the history of a mind who's basic theme is captured in the simple statement, ". . . the religion of Christ ought to be, and was meant to be, to its possessors, not something to make them miserable, but something to make them happy . . . ."

The first step to be taken on this spiritual journey toward a happy Christian life, is to believe with all of our *will* that Jesus Christ is Lord and Savior, and able to release us from the dominion of sin. The Bible is forever expounding this truth, and Hannah Whitall Smith is very capable of helping the reader to find passages from Scripture supporting this claim. One such passage is when the angel appeared unto Joseph in a dream and proclaimed the coming birth of Jesus by saying, "And thou shalt save his people from their sins." Another selection used by H.W.S. is the time when Peter was preaching on the porch of the Temple to the wandering Jews saying, "Unto you first, God, having raised up his Son Jesus, sent him to bless you in turning away everyone of you from his infirmities."

After being assured of Scriptural reference for support, we discover in our search for a higher Christian life the magnificence of God's love. This love is *power*, and when we begin to have some glimpses of this gift, we must turn from our weaknesses, putting our trust into God's hands, and trusting Him to deliver us. Hannah Whitall Smith concerns herself with the difficulty that may arise in our spiritual quest if there is misunderstanding between our part, which is to trust, and God's part, which is to work. In the higher life the believer can do nothing but trust, while the Lord in whom he trusts does the work, i.e., transforms his mind so that he may know what is the good, acceptable and perfect will of

God. To clarify this process, H.W.S. uses the following illustration:

> ... Suppose I were to describe to a person who was entirely ignorant of the subject the way in which a lump of clay is made into a beautiful vessel. I tell him first the part of the clay in the matter; and all I can say about this is that the clay is put into the potter's hands, and then lies passive there, submitting itself to all the turnings and overturnings of the potter's hands upon it. There is really nothing else to be said about the clay's part. But could my hearer argue from this that nothing else is done because I say that this is all the clay can do? If he is an intelligent hearer he will not dream of doing so, but will say, "I understand; this is what the clay must do. But what must the potter do?: "Ah," I answer, "now we come to the important part. The potter takes the clay thus abandoned to his working, and begins to mold and fashion it according to his own will. He kneads and works it; he tears it apart and presses it together again; he wets it and then suffers it to dry. Sometimes he works at it for hours together; sometimes he lays it aside for days, and does not touch it. And then, when by all these processes he has made it perfectly pliable in his hands, he proceeds to make it up into the vessel he had proposed. He turns it upon the wheel, planes it and smooths it, and dries it in the sun, bakes it in the oven, and finally turns it out of his workshop, a vessel to his honor and fit for his use.[10]

Now that H.W.S. has established Scripture as the basis for the Christian's "higher life," and distinguished humanity's side and God's side in the process of sanctification, she sets out to discuss the chief characteristics of "the life hid with Christ in God," and how it is different from the ordinary Christian life. The ordinary life of the Christian is a struggle, for he continues to try and manage his own affairs. In the higher life he finds victory over sin and inward rest for the soul because he lets the Lord carry his burdens. Again, Hannah Whitall

Smith uses the vehicle of illustration to make her point:
> Most Christians are like a man who was toiling along the road, bending under a heavy burden, when a wagon overtook him, and the driver kindly offered to help him on his journey. He joyfully accepted the offer but when seated in the wagon, continued to bend beneath his burden, which he still kept on his shoulders. "Why do you not lay down your burden?" asked the kind-hearted driver. "Oh!" replied the man, "I feel that it is almost too much to ask you to carry me, and I could not think of letting you carry my burden too." And so Christians, who have given themselves into the care and keeping of the Lord Jesus still continue to bend beneath the weight of their burdens, and often go weary and heavy-laden throughout the whole length of their journey.[11]

To be burden free releases us for Christian ministry and spiritual development. The Good news of Jesus Christ, as interpreted by H.W.S., is that we can have perfect peace in this life of imperfection, and trust in God is the key to its attainment.

The author experienced in her life the immediate revelation of God which convinced her, beyond all doubt, that He can be found, and is a resting place of absolute peace and joy. She reached out her hand and received an answering clasp. This mystical perception brought her a solemn assurance, a tranquility, an ever present help in trouble, and a spirit of happiness which verified her faith and validated her beliefs. She became convinced that this revelation is a gift of God in Christ Jesus that cannot be earned or attained, but only received as we ask for it. God bestows this gift upon those who are absolutely committed to giving their lives to Him and trusting in Him without any reservations. The *will* thus becomes very important in this journey to attain the higher life, and in order to emphasize the importance of abandonment and trust, Mrs. Smith affirms in a statement of faith what she means:

"Lord Jesus, I believe that thou art able and willing to deliver me from all the care and unrest and bondage of my Christian life. I believe thou didst care to set me free, not only in the future, but now and here. I believe you art stronger than sin, and that thou canst keep me, even me, in my extreme of weakness, from falling into its snares or yielding obedience to its commands. And Lord, I am going to trust thee to keep me. I have tried keeping myself, and have failed, most grievously. I am absolutely helpless. So now I will trust thee. I give myself to thee. I keep no reserves. Body, soul and spirit I present myself to thee as a piece of clay, to be fashioned into anything thy love and thy wisdom shall choose. And now I am thine. I believe thou dost accept that which I present to thee; I believe that this poor, weak foolish heart has been taken possession of by thee, and that thou hast even at this very moment begun to work in me to will and to do of thy good pleasure. I trust thee utterly, and I trust thee now."[12]

Since temptations and doubts are sure to beset us upon entering the higher Christian life, we are bound to experience difficulties. As one moves from the joy of consecration to the difficulties following the making of this commitment, he is most bothered by the question of feelings. Since one cannot see, hear, or feel a faith commitment, the Christian pilgrim might have a hard time assuring himself that what has happened in his life is real. But there is no room in the life hid with Christ in God for this kind of unsettled doubt. What you must do is ask God to reveal any hidden rebellion within yourself, and if He reveals nothing, then you must believe that your surrender is complete. To continue in uncertain doubt is to prevent spiritual growth, and H.W.S. has no patience for those who continue to argue the matter after this point.

Since being firm with oneself is most important in the type of faith development that Hannah Whitall Smith has here outlined, she stresses, once again, the importance of the *will.* If we continue to burden our thoughts with questions, such as whether or not we have *really* surrendered ourselves, we shall stifle our growth. We must be willing to accept by faith that it happened. This is one of the major themes of this Quaker classic — the belief that we can control and set our will into conformity with God's Will. If we are able to "set our faces like flint to carry out His will," all else in the higher life will follow.

In the style of a true Quaker mystic, Hannah Whitall Smith stresses the need to use the interior eyes of our understanding in our walk with God. In the life hid with Christ in God we are able to see the eternal in the midst of time, and feel the infinite here in the finite. She knew of the spiritual experience that comes to life when through our inward eyes we are given a glimpse into eternal reality. She was able to see with new eyes and catch intimations of the divine presence, where most of us are blind. But as our teacher, she seeks to take us where we have not been, and show us a life that we did not think possible. She moves us into regions of the spirit that expand our thought and lift us, through the will, to the higher life. Once thought to be a life reserved for saints, she invites us, every man and woman, into this enlightened interior life.

As we seek to discern guidance for our spiritual journey, H.W.S., in the true fashion of 19th Century Quakerism, is very guarded when it comes to the use of reason. The very first moment that we clearly see something to be correct is always the moment to act. She writes:

> If we 'let in the reasoner,' as the Quakers express it, the golden opportunity is lost, and obedience becomes more and more difficult with every moment's delay. The old self-will wakens into life; and the energies that should have been occupied with obeying are

absorbed instead in the struggle with doubts and reasonings.[13]

Here again she expresses her firmness of attitude on the will, and uses military terminology to make her point: "Our fight is to be a fight of faith," she expounds, "and the moment we let in doubts, our fight ceases, and our rebellion begins."[14]

Hannah Whitall Smith believed, as did the writers of Scripture, that the Christian life throughout is a warfare between the forces of God and the forces of evil. Since she believed that the Christian seeking the higher life must accept temptation to sin as an enemy with which to contend, one should not be discouraged because he is still tempted after his conversion to the life hid with Christ in God. This is to be expected. If the Christian seeker becomes discouraged, then the real problem is not that he is tempted, but that he becomes discouraged when he is tempted. This must not be allowed to happen, for we must, by an act of the will, put our trust in the guidance of God to lead us on to greater heights in our spiritual journey.

The difficulties associated with reaching these greater heights of the spirit cannot be avoided, but we can control our attitude toward them. As we experience failure we must immediately look for the reason behind our defeat, and H.W.S. suggests that we look for the cause in the strength of the sin committed, and for a weakness within the self that would allow the defeat to occur. She suggests the following prayer to help prevent failure or discover its cause:

> Search me, O God, and know my heart; try me and know my thoughts; and see if there be any wicked way in me, and lead me in the way everlasting.[15]

The "way everlasting" in mystical terminology, is the way to God through the human soul. This way is open or closed to each individual person as he or she learns how to use the key that opens the door to the Eternal in his own inner life. This way is not controlled by a stern sense of duty, where the soul obeys God from fear of punishment, but the way of Hannah Whitall Smith is, instead, controlled by an inward-life principle that works out the will of the Divine-Life giver in love, without fear. H.W.S. uses an illustration to help the reader differentiate between the religion of legality, performed with a stern sense of duty, and the religion of grace, controlled by the principle of love within:

> The religion of legality is as though a man should decide to have an apple orchard, and should try to make one by first getting some apples of the kind desired, and then getting roots to fasten to the trunk, and finally purchasing a field in which to plant his manufactured tree. That is, first the fruit, second the branches, third the root, fourth the field. But the religion of grace follows a different order. It begins at the root, and grows up, and blossoms out into flowers and fruit.[16]

To be a Christian in the "higher life," requires that we accept the yoke of Christ, not as a yoke of bondage, but as a yoke of liberation. We must believe Christ when he speaks to us through the Scripture and says: "My yoke is easy and my burden is light." To be at liberty in Him, instead of in bondage to Him, releases within us the servant spirit, and is replaced by the spirit of service.

To make Christ the agent of our lives is to surrender our hearts to Him, not because we have to, but because we want to. There is joy in obedience, which is the fruit that we bring forth from the life of devotion to Him, and at this point we no longer live for ourselves, but as wholly dedicated servants of God. Our acknowledgment of joy in this dramatic change of lifestyle is followed by Divine Union, and in this book all steps suggested by H.W.S. lead to this union where we become one with Jesus Christ.

In a dramatic announcement, Hannah Whitall Smith

shares with her readers the "good news" of the "Christ Within:"

> Dear friend, I make the glad announcement to thee that the Lord is in thy heart. Since the day of thy conversion He has been dwelling there, but thou hast lived on in ignorance of it. Every moment during all that time might have been passed in the sunshine of His sweet presence, and every step have been taken under His advice. But because thou knew it not, and did not look for Him there, thy life has been lonely and full of failure. But now that I make the announcement to thee, how wilt thou receive it? Art thou glad to have Him? Wilt thou throw wide open every door to welcome Him in? Wilt thou joyfully and thankfully give up the government of thy life into His hands? Wilt thou consult Him about everything, and let Him decide each step for thee, and mark out every path? Wilt thou invite Him into thy innermost chambers, and make Him the sharer in thy most hidden life? Wilt thou say "Yes" to all His longing for union with thee, and with a glad and eager abandonment hand thyself and all that concerns thee over into His hands? If thou wilt, then shall thy soul begin to know something of the joy of union with Christ.[17]

The basis of all Quaker belief rests on this principle of "the Christ within," and is, indeed, their most unique contribution to Christian theology. The joy of learning this exciting fact brings the Christian pilgrim to a new height of experience and understanding. The doctrine of the "Inner Light of Christ," first expounded by George Fox 325 years ago, was revolutionary for Seventeenth Century England, and continues to be just as fresh and exciting for the Christian seeker when he discovers this principle at work in his life today. To understand the concept of Christ within you, is to prepare the way for the emergence of the Divine Union. The union of human with Divine causes us to "mount up with wings as eagles," for the higher life is the life on wings. Our souls were made to never be satisfied with anything short of flying, as H.W.S. illustrates:

> Like the captive-born eagle that feels within it the instinct of flight, and chafes and frets at its imprisonment, hardly knowing what it longs for, so do our souls chafe and fret, and cry out for freedom. We can never rest on earth, and we long to "fly away" from all that so holds and hampers and imprisons us here.[18]

The promise has been given to us:
> "They that wait upon the Lord SHALL mount up with wings as eagles." Not "may perhaps mount up," but "SHALL." It is the inevitable result. May we each one prove it for ourselves![19]

With these words we come to the close of our inward pilgrimage through *The Christian's Secret Of A Happy Life*. The orderly step by step developmental process through which Hannah Whitall Smith leads us is difficult, yet easy, hard, yet simple. This is the paradox of the Christian faith, for on the one hand the message is clear and simple, but on the other hand it is difficult and demanding. Both of these statements are true. *The Christian's Secret Of A Happy Life* offers us the opportunity to share in the joy of committed Christian living, but at the same time it promises a pathway strewn with obstacles toward its achievement. We cannot expect the way to be easy, although the message is simple. Hannah Whitall Smith came to her understanding about life after traveling through some difficult periods of spiritual adjustment, but she finally came to the realization that the Christian life is meant to be happy, and she has brought to us a wealth of spiritual insight from her personal journey. For her the most important element in the religious life is the *will*. If one can bring his will into accord with the will of God, and remain strong throughout the trials and temptations of life, then, according to H.W.S., he is on the road toward a happy Christian life. The heart, the mind and the will are all important in the life of the religious pilgrim, but for Mrs. Smith, the greatest of these is the *will*.

How Christlike Hannah Whitall Smith became during the course of her pilgrimage is exemplified in this beautifully written reflection from the Light of Christ. It illustrates how great she grew in gentleness, how simple in prayer, and how expectantly she waited upon the Lord in the silence of the Quaker Meeting. From the silence of worship and the turmoil of living, came an inner peace and simplicity that radiated in abundant warmth and eagerness to share her secret of a happy Christian life. She was an obedient servant, always willing to give, share, and teach her faith. This was her distinct mission, and how well she performed it can be measured by the thousands of disciples who have lived, and are now living a happy Christian life as a result of her efforts.

As we continue our inward pilgrimage through these Quaker classics, we shall remember the beautiful simplicity and practical application of Hannah Whitall Smith's important literary contribution. She has demonstrated, by example, that the Christian life is not a sober, dull existence, but a joyful experience that by its very nature is evangelical in message, and apostolic in fervor. In her own dark century it was a rare experience to hear an optimistic Gospel message, and to discover the Good News that religion is to be a joyous affair. Through the printed word she has been able to spread this important message to thousands who are in search of a Christian faith that is strong enough to withstand probing questions, and hopeful enough to dispel the mood of hopelessness that has taken over so much of our current outlook on life. By following the way suggested in this classic, we can rejoice with H.W.S. in a Christianity that knows no intellectual snobbery, no social superiority and no temperamental privilege. By following the way of Mrs. Smith, we discover that Christianity is not some vague philosophy, but a way of life. As a result of her testimony, our way becomes more enlightened, our burdens become more bearable, our hope becomes more durable, and our joy in the celebration of life becomes contagious.

Notes: Chapter III

[1] Bertrand Russell, *Mysticism and Logic* (Doubleday & Co., 1957), p. 45.
[2] Ibid., p. 54.
[3] Logan Pearsall Smith, *A Religious Rebel* (London: Nisbet & Co., Ltd., 1949), p. 135.
[4] Logan Pearsall Smith, *Unforgotten Years* (Boston: Little Brown & Co., 1939), p. 44-45.
[5] Ibid., p. 47-48.
[6] Ibid., p. 96-97.
[7] Jessamyn West, *The Quaker Reader* (New York: The Viking Press, 1962), p. 333-334.
[8] Ibid., p. 337.
[9] Hannah Whitall Smith, *The Christian's Secret of a Happy Life*, (Old Tappan, New Jersey: The Revell Co., 1942), p. 13.
[10] Ibid., p. 23-24.
[11] Ibid., p. 28.
[12] Ibid., p. 39-40.
[13] Ibid., p. 72.
[14] Ibid., p. 77.
[15] Ibid., p. 100.
[16] Ibid., p. 114.
[17] Ibid., p. 157-158.
[18] Ibid., p. 166.
[19] Ibid., p. 174.

Chapter IV

Rufus M. Jones: Interpreter of the Inward Way

"His message is amazingly timeless, but that means that it is amazingly timely."

— Harry Emerson Fosdick

In the study of these Quaker classics of devotion, we can see the changing aspects of one continuing process. All of the reflections from the Light of Christ which we have already studied reveal both a search and its outcome. All can be generally described as a search for God, and how that search was actualized.

We began with William Penn, whose *Fruits Of Solitude* mark an important transition in the history of the Society of Friends. He was a liberator in two important respects, since he not only worked toward political liberation by establishing the free Colony of Pennsylvania, but he also sought to free people spiritually from antiquated ideas about God, and led them to a new experience of the Living Christ.

In our study of John Woolman and his *Journal,* we discovered how moral idealism could be transferred to practical action, thus enabling him to demonstrate the Quaker ideal better than any other individual. His search for God was lived out in his actions with his fellowmen. He not only sought, but he found, thus helping to lay the foundations for our own spiritual pilgrimage.

The spiritual forces at work in William Penn and John

Woolman were also active in the life of Hannah Whitall Smith. H.W.S. has borne witness to the importance of the *will* in the religious life. Her search was one of travail, but when she entered the period of the higher life she became centered upon love, devotion, and obedience to God. Her testimony is one of encouragement to all who seek a life of unity with the Living Christ.

The quest continues through the author of *The Double Search*. Few persons have surpassed Rufus Jones in raising the spiritual vision of humanity. Like a light out of darkness, he has been able to ignite the candles of spiritual seekers for decades, and with his knowledge of mysticism and his practical experience in the life of the Spirit, he has helped a generation of religious *spectators* become *participants*. Throughout his lifetime he undertook the task of working out for humanity a religion of life, rooted in the eternal nature of the Spirit of God and the spirit of man. This task produced the Quaker classic of devotion here discussed, and all of his other masterpieces of literature.

No other Friend since John Woolman has had as much influence on the life and thought of American Quakerism as Rufus Jones. This Quaker philosopher from Haverford College was able to interpret for himself, the Society of Friends, and the whole of Christendom, a mysticism which was Christ-centered and action oriented. Like the other Quaker authors discussed in this volume, he understood the need for a mysticism that did not induce the individual seeker into a monastic withdrawal from society, but prepared the seeker, instead, to live a Christian life within his society. He always made a distinction between affirmative mysticism and negative mysticism. Negative mysticism called for withdrawal from the world, while affirmative mysticism seeks a union with God without the loss of individual personality in the world. Rufus Jones was a mystic of the affirmative type, seeking to reach God

directly without ever losing touch with the world and his concern for humanity. Elizabeth Gray Vining writes on this important distinction in her biography on Rufus Jones, entitled, *Friend Of Life:*
> A mysticism, however lofty, which left humanity behind, was foreign to Rufus Jones' thought. 'I am interested,' he said, 'in a mysticism which brings life to its full rich goal of complete living, with radiance and joy and creative power.' A mysticism, furthermore, that did not find expression in creative service, remained to him incomplete. In describing John Woolman, who was to him the best expression of the ideal of Quaker mysticism, he told how Woolman became extraordinarily tender to human need and sensitive to 'every breath of wrong' which man does to man. 'Here was a mysticism,' he concluded, 'and it was the type to which I dedicated my life — which sought no ecstasies, no miracles of levitation, no startling phenomena, no private raptures, but whose over-mastering passion was to turn all he possessed, including his own life, 'into the channel of universal love.'[1]

As one studies the life of Rufus Jones, he becomes aware of a man whose life was made of many facets, yet they were all interwoven into the fabric of mysticism. His explanation of mysticism included *a Biblical foundation, a Christ-centered approach toward its interpretation, intellectual content,* and *a Christian understanding of service.*

Rufus Jones was born on a farm in South China, Maine, January 25, 1863. In *A Boy's Religion From Memory,* he writes: "I came into a world where love was waiting for me, and into a family in which religion was as important an element for life as was the air we breathed."[2] He was not christened in a church, but he writes: "I was sprinkled from morning till night with the dew of religion. We never ate a meal which did not begin with a hush of Thanksgiving, we never began a day without a family gathering, the reading of a chapter in the Bible, followed by a period of silent worship when we talked with God, not far away, but very near. This was a Quaker home, the product of generations of deep inward religious life."[3]

Since young Rufus grew up in an environment similar to most farm boys in Maine, he had to work hard chopping wood, raking hay, and doing countless other tasks required by farm living. The only trips away from the serene setting of South China were the occasional journeys to Augusta to sell farm produce, and purchase needed supplies. Much of his leisure time was spent in study, but there were few books at home. Because of this lack of literature, he devoted hours at a time reading the one book most readily available and approved by his parents for his reading — The Bible. He was able to recite long passages by heart, and the Biblical characters, he relates, "were more a part of me than movie actors or baseball heroes ever can be to a modern youth." From his early childhood the Bible played an important part in his development, and as he began to write and deliver addresses, he would use verses of Scripture to bring power to his messages, which would flow naturally from his tongue or pen. As he grew spiritually and developed his special understanding of Christian mysticism, the Bible became foundational in its formulation.

In modern times some Christian scholars have criticized Rufus Jones for not being Christocentric in his interpretation of mysticism. He is certainly not as evangelical as Hannah Whitall Smith, but to say that Christ was not the center around which his religious life evolved is a misstatement. Christ was at the heart of his life and thought. He writes about his Christocentric faith in his book, *The Eternal Gospel:* "I owe more to Christ for my unswerving conviction of the reality of God than to anything else in the universe. Whenever I find my way back to Him and really *see* Him living his marvellous life of love and trust and confidence and fellowship with God, I rise up in the strength of it and catch from Him a contagion of faith which is more than an anchor to the soul in the storm; it becomes a driving power that sends one forth to help build the Kingdom of God here and now."[4]

Rufus Jones saw Christ as the visible expression of God. He writes: "Christ has changed for us the whole atmosphere of religious life and thought. The words he used for God and about God may perhaps all have been used before in one setting or another. But what never happened before was that no one had felt as he did in his relation to God. No one before had so consciously 'belonged' in intimate fellowship with God."[5] It was only through Christ that Rufus Jones was able to believe in a God so personal and loving, so great and so good, that he could call Him Father. For him Christ was more than an historical personality, He was an inward reality, and the Center around which his understanding of mysticism was rooted and integrated.

For Rufus Jones, the Christian life demanded academic excellence. Before he came to Haverford to teach, this Quaker school had already established itself as a leader among colleges emphasizing the importance of hard, disciplined study. Rufus Jones fit well in this type of academic setting, and stressed the need for reasoning power within his structure of mystical religion. He warned against a religion that was all feeling with no constructive principle of interpretation. This, to him, was one of the major threats to the Christian faith, for without a structure and content of thought, Christianity could degenerate into mere emotionalism, with no defense other than the experience of each individual. The mysticism which Rufus Jones interpreted is more than just individual *feeling*, it is living the life of the Christian scholar, and this requires *study*. He recognized that developing the rational side of the Christian faith is important in living a balanced Christian life. If we are to understand Rufus Jones' interpretation of mysticism, we must see this aspect clearly, since this emphasis added direction to his religious thought.

The concept of Christian service made the mysticism of Rufus Jones practical. In the introduction to his book *Practical Christianity,* he writes: "Christianity is not Christianity until it is applied to life. It cannot be reduced to a bloodless theory, an abstract scheme any more than a pressed flower can be a genuine violet. It must not stop short of its purpose, which is as a vital force, to reconstruct man and society and to work out as a fact the Spirit of Jesus Christ in the individual, and in the social organism."[6]

Rufus Jones was a tireless worker for concerns which promoted human dignity and social justice. He was the founding father of the American Friends Service Committee, and in his closing remarks at the twenty-fifth anniversary celebration of the AFSC, Rufus Jones shared his understanding of Christian responsibility to help relieve the burdens of others: ". . . God won't do it if we don't help him. If it isn't for human hands and human lips, and the human heart to touch it and help bear this burden, it won't be done."

In the winter of 1938, Rufus Jones and two other Friends made a much publicized voyage to Germany. Their mission was to visit Adolf Hitler, and try to persuade him to speed the emigration of the German Jewish population who were under severe persecution. Though their mission to many observers seemed naive, and lacking in understanding of the "ways of the world," to Rufus Jones and his companions this was practical Christianity in action, and they felt that as long as there was the slightest chance of making a difference for the good, they had to go. In the end they were not able to see Hitler, but they did get to see

Richard Heydrich, head of the Gestapo. Their simple statement of purpose was given to one of his subordinates which reads, as summarized by Daisy Newman in *A Procession Of Friends:* "We represent no governments, no international organizations, no parties, no sects and we have no interest in propaganda... We were the first to arrive in Vienna after the War. We do not ask who is to blame... Our task is to support life and to suffer with those who are suffering."[7]

A mysticism that has a biblical foundation, is Christ-centered, intellectually sound, and service oriented, is what Rufus Jones sought and developed in his own Christian life. He does not counsel withdrawal from the world, but, instead, urges Christian penetration of it. He does not teach a mysticism that draws one away from Christ, he makes Christ the very center of the mystical experience. This new understanding of what it means to be a mystic in the Christian tradition, offers the individual seeker a sense of the Divine in a finite world of action. It means that the human vehicle has the capacity to feel the power and presence of God breaking forth into our existence, and illuminating the true meaning of life.

Rufus Jones has given assistance to those who seek to understand him by producing several volumes of an autobiographical character. Instead of writing a single autobiography, Jones wrote, *A Boy's Religion From Memory, Finding The Trail Of Life, The Trail Of Life In College,* and *The Trail Of Life In The Middle Years.* He is especially helpful in referring to his effort to discover what he called his "life-clue." As he worked toward the completion of his final year in college, Jones was summoned to Philadelphia by a successful merchant to discuss the possibility of a career in law, for which this philanthropic man was willing to pay. For a brief time Rufus Jones was overwhelmed by what seemed to be a "providential provision" for his future career, but later, as he sat alone in his college study a new turn in his life began to take form. Jones describes what happened next:

> ... I slowly saw, at first dimly and then more clearly, that I could not accept it. I could not have told then, with explicit reasons, precisely WHY I could not take this generous provision. I saw my way only as migrating birds see their way, but I *felt* the line of direction grow steadily more and more plain. Again and again in my life I have had something surge into my consciousness, some guiding light break in, when momentous decisions have had to be made. One may call it 'an opening,' or 'an inner light' or a 'Socratic daimon,' or 'the deeper accumulated wisdom of the subconscious life,' or by any other name that is current. Dim lines of light appear in the darkness and as I wait quietly centered down into communion with the deeper life within me *I see the way to go.*
>
> Before the night was over I was convinced that I should not study law and that that profession was not to be my career. It did not mean that it was not a worthy career; only that some other line of life was better *for me* .... With what wisdom of phrase I could command I wrote my generous friend and told him that I was unable to accept his offer, and that my mind was unexpectedly moving in a different direction for my career in life. I may conclude the incident by saying that we became more close than ever in our appreciation of one another and our friendship lasted without a flaw or break unto his death.[8]

Besides making this important decision not to pursue a career in law, another choice during this last year at Haverford had a far-reaching affect on his future life's work. For students to be granted a degree from Haverford, a "graduating thesis" had to be written by every prospective graduate. Rufus Jones went to his beloved professor, Pliny Earle Chase, and discussed at great length what his topic for this paper should be. His teacher suggested the subject, "Mysticism and its Exponents," and young Jones eagerly agreed. He writes about this momentous work, and tells how important it was to his future career:

> There are some passages in the thesis which I have quite emphatically outgrown, but I am surprised at the number of ideas and insights in that old thesis which have remained with me still alive and vital until the present time.
>
> It is however, in most ways unimportant now whether the thesis was on right lines or on wrong lines; the significant point to note is that I had here found the field of my life work. Hereafter all my reading and thinking and research work bore directly or indirectly on some phase of mysticism. Everything carried me on in this direction and many features of my later life, up to the present moment, have been determined by that early decision to write a graduating thesis on Mysticism.[9]

The Florentine Machiavelli wrote the following in his *Discourses On Livy:* "All religions must be again and again rejuvenated by a return to their original principle." The Society of Friends arose in Puritan England as a living hope, whose main purpose was the recovery of Basic Christianity. The times called loudly for a religion of experience, an intimate life with God, for a religion more simple, practical, social, in a word, more Christlike, than the established church, or any other movements of the day. The People called Quakers, however, did not intend to start something new, but, instead, to *recover* a vitality that had been lost. Since Rufus Jones interpreted Christian history as a Quaker mystic, he believed that the original idea of the church had become distorted over the years, showing little resemblance to what it had started out to be. He observed little correlation between the church now, and the organic spiritual fellowship which the church was in the beginning. Basic Christianity was an organic body that was held together by a common experience with the

73

Living Christ, and since it was a mystical group, guided by gifted persons and not ordained officials, it followed perfectly the Pauline idea of "Christ's body." Its entire method of organization was designed to help persons encounter the Holy Spirit in an inward mystical experience.

Something happened, however, to change this vital cell of Spiritual activity. Forces from the outside were pushing in on the early Christians, and giving them no choice except to develop a plan of survival. Gnosticism was an increasing problem, and the history of Early Church organization, after this exciting apostolic period, can be seen chiefly as a response to this threatening cult. Creeds were formed, and the one bishop system became a necessity if the powers of the church were to be centralized to meet the outward threats. Long before the New Testament Canon was closed, a rigid contrived organization was smothering the spiritual fellowship of the Early Christians.

Various philosophical influences from the outside were bound to change the character of Christianity. Individual mysticism like that of Plotinus and St. Augustine became dominant, and although the contributions of these scholars concerning the life in the spirit is important, it lacks the vitality of the group experience that was inherent at the beginning of the Christian movement. This was a more intellectual form of mysticism, and stressed the need for solitary worship.

Rufus Jones saw the People called Quakers as the one group in the history of the Christian church that is actually working to revive Primitive Christianity. It is the best historical example of a mystical body with an organization as loose as the Early Church, designed to promote mystical experience. In the formative years of the young movement, Friends encouraged a group mysticism, discounting externals, and basing its existence on an inward authority. Quakers discovered that, as great as individual mystical awareness is, group mysticism is even greater. Early Friends have testified to the life and power received in this group mystical experience in a variety of ways, but all agree to a basic theme. This foundational revelation was that Christ is present NOW — "He has come to teach his followers himself!" This exciting discovery amidst the bland background of Puritanism, caused a storm of Quaker testimony. When his great experience of the soul occurred, Isaac Penington declared: "This is He, this is He. There is no other. This is He whom I have waited for and sought after from my childhood. I have met with my God; I have met with my Saviour. I have felt the healings drop upon my soul from under His wings." Fox himself wrote that he "knew God experimentally," and had "a key that did open." Early Friends, like Early Christians, urged all persons to "return home.... Within!"

Since the Society of Friends arose in Seventeenth Century England to recover what had been lost, and to revive the Christian church from within, they were not interested in becoming just another sect. If there was one thing that Puritan England did not need it was another fanatical fringe group practicing a limited religion within a closed sect. This was not the intention of Fox, Barclay, Penn, or any of the other important founders of the Quaker movement. Instead, these Friends saw their mission and the work of the Society of Friends as much larger. They were involved in nothing less than the recovery of Basic Christianity.

In silence, without rite or symbol, they experienced the "Light of Christ Within," and soon discovered that external sacraments or even the Bible were not necessary for this experience with the Living Christ. There were no fixed creeds of belief; no pattern or ritual of worship that had to be followed; no formal prayers to be prayed; no benedictions to be pronounced. George

Fox, with his simple doctrine of experiential Christianity, liberated thousands of persons from the shadow of past dogma, and led them into the bright sunlight of encounter with the Living Christ. This was the "Good News" of Quakerism, and it shone as a bright light in a day when religion was formal and dull.

Two-hundred and fifty years after this Quaker explosion, Rufus Jones became the Society of Friends' most able spokesman. After two and a half centuries of spiritual activity, the People called Quakers had become beset with internal bickering. The loose band of hearty spiritual reformers who travelled throughout Europe and America in the Seventeenth and Eighteenth centuries, had become a tired lot in the Nineteenth and Twentieth centuries. They were more concerned with Quaker tradition than with the recovery of Basic Christianity. The People called Quakers had become Quaker*ism*, and the history of the Movement reflected a deep need for spiritual uplift, as well as a guide to lead them back to their original purpose.

In Rufus Jones the Society of Friends was given their beacon of light. History shows that just when times are the darkest, then is the greatest hope. Rufus Jones came on the Quaker scene when he was most needed, and contributed a new direction to Quaker rational thinking. He was able to relate the Quaker faith to the new discoveries in psychology, showing that as individuals we are organic wholes — mentally, spiritually, and physically. Associated with this teaching, he preached the doctrine of "the conjunct life," or that God and man are conjunct. His contributions to Quaker Christian thought are numerous, and his books are important testimonies of the soul, expressing a wholistic Christian mysticism that can serve us as a model.

As Rufus Jones studied and meditated about the different aspects of Quakerism, he discovered that they were all interrelated. This discovery grew as he developed his understanding of the conjunct life, and the spiritual unity of the person occupied much of his time and thought. As his philosophy was being formed into a mature understanding of Basic Christianity, he could no longer talk about the "Light of Christ Within," without mentioning where this Light is nourished. No longer could he talk about worship without mentioning the source of this spiritual exercise, and the logical outgrowth in service to the world. No longer could he speak about Quaker service without mentioning the roots out of which this concern for service arose. He preached a sacramental view of life and a wholistic faith, and made the important personal discovery that the vital aspects of Basic Christianity cannot be separated from each other.

The logical outgrowth of this wholistic understanding is discovered within the pages of *The Double Search*. If Basic Christianity is a wholistic faith, then man and God are conjunct. Since Rufus Jones saw the basic problem in the Christian religion as an inconsistency at the heart of its thinking, he sought to abolish the main point of difficulty, which was the dualistic understanding of God and humans which had developed over the past two-thousand years. As long as we believe that we are *here* and God is out *there* somewhere, unrelated to us, then we cannot unite our thinking. We must begin again, not with two divided entities, but with one indivisible experience in which God and persons are interrelated. The important word here is *experience,* and it is the most important word in the language of Basic Christianity. If we value the religious experiences of persons through the ages, and our own experience now, we are forced to the undeniable conclusion that we are involved in a double search. Only through the verification of experience are we brought to this exciting understanding.

All of the great mystics in history insist that "the soul

standeth in God." Through atonement God is reaching out to us, and through prayer we are reaching out to God. In the *experience*, the human and divine meet. The seed of God is always ready to be nourished and brought to flower, and as we come to our actual selves, we speak of God. This seed is never separated from us, but it can lie dormant in the midst of selfish greed, inhumanity, injustice and anger. In the very foundation of our souls we know that these things are wrong, and if we do not know the distinction between good and evil, then we have not developed the seed within us, and can rightly be called "moral imbeciles."

Since truth, beauty, justice and love are the real goals of our actual selves, we best exemplify our humanity when, in our search for God, we are working for ideals that lift us out of the level of things, and proclaim a spiritual order of what might be. In a higher realm of the spirit we become conjunct with God in a great mystical experience, and we discover what ought to be, before it is built. As Rufus Jones has said, "The Kingdom of God is a vision in a soul before it is an accomplished fact of history."[10]

We do not rise to the level of spiritual awareness, of which we are capable, when we reduce our heritage as persons, and make what is or what has been the measure of our humanity. We should never stop at the end of what is visible. Rufus Jones calls us to reach beyond the *seen* to the *unseen*, and urges us to use our "invisible eyes" to capture glimpses of a reality that bids us to grow and live on the mountaintop of *what ought to be*. To live beyond the *what is* and enter the frontiers of the spirit is the challenge to all, for we are ideal-forming persons.

As humans we are constantly moving from level to level, for we are not one strata beings. We know the feelings of anger and hatred, but we also have appreciation for beauty, convictions of truth, and experiences of love and justice. It is by these spiritual realities that we are called to live. They are revealed in us by an objective reality and point us to a spiritual world above the level of matter. When the soul experiences these greater visions, he or she bears testimony to the Source of these realities.

Since the Quaker classics are testimonies of the soul concerning the validity of direct religious experience, they express the actual foundations on which the Christian faith is built. They verify the existence of a Living God, by direct experience. *The Double Search* is an important part of this testimony, for it helps us to realize more clearly than any other testimony, that God is Spirit and is the larger Spirit of our own finite spirits. The faith of Rufus Jones is not a "pie in the sky" religion, but, instead, a faith with primary concern for the development of the inner self. He writes: "God is to be found and known, not in terms of astronomy, but rather in terms of our noblest ethical and spiritual aspirations.... To find Him we do not need to travel off into space or backward in time, but rather to go down to profounder levels of spiritual life."[11]

In order to fully understand the wholistic Christian faith of Rufus Jones, we must begin with his understanding of the historical and inward Christ, and ask the important question, "How are they related?" It is to this question that Dr. Jones addresses himself in the first chapter of *The Double Search*. For him, the Christ of history was the physical illumination of the "Light of Christ" found in the spiritual depths of each human being. For a Quaker like Rufus Jones, the Prologue of John's Gospel holds special significance in his understanding of this connection. In the historical Christ the "Word became flesh." He came into the world to teach supreme truths about ourselves as humans, and to teach supreme truths about God, whom he called "Father." William Temple shared this profound understanding when he said: " 'What is God like?' The answer to that question is 'Christ.' And when we ask, 'what is humanity?' we look at Christ to find the answer." In Christ the human and divine were perfectly formed to reveal an important reality. This means that we can no longer talk about the God-likeness of Christ, but, instead, the Christ-likeness of God! And when we as humans are looking for a model, we must turn to Christ, for in him our full humanity is given expression.

In the book, *Religious Foundations,* Rufus Jones consolidates the teaching of Jesus into four important truths: 1) God as Father, 2) that men and women are potential sons and daughters of God, 3) the Kingdom of God means a new order in social life, and 4) Jesus raised life to an eternal quality, and taught that all life is sacred. In these four basic teachings, Rufus Jones captured the purpose for Jesus Christ's entry into the physical world. However, Dr. Jones makes clear that one more basic teaching must be mentioned in order to fully understand the purpose of Christ. In everything that Jesus said and did, he used the unconventional method of *love*. Self-sacrificing love for others permeated his whole being, and brought his followers to a new understanding of what it means to be human. Since Christ, who was finally killed by hate, knew that the way of love could only be brought into our world by love, he suffered in order to reach his followers with this new and exciting message. He knew that if the world was going to be changed to his way of thinking, he could not count his physical life valuable. He accepted the personal tragic outcome of this thinking, but as a result ushered into our world a doctrine of self-giving love that, if followed, would raise humanity to new levels of spiritual insight.

Rufus Jones believed in the resurrection of Jesus Christ, and accepted in full the belief that the Holy Spirit is the Christ of history continuing to reveal himself. He interpreted the Christ within as the same historical Christ who is revealing himself to people today, just as he revealed himself to Peter and James under the Syrian Blue. Dr. Jones writes:

> The procession of the Holy Ghost is a continuous revelation and exhibition of Christ within men. Whether we use the expression Holy Spirit or Christ within or Spiritual Christ, we mean God operating upon human spirits and consciously witnessed and appreciated in them.[12]

In the second and third chapters of *The Double Search,* Professor Jones discusses the *Atonement-*God's search for us, and *Prayer-*our search for God. As a prelude to these important chapters in the thought of the author, he introduces his understanding of "the conjunct life" in his book, *Social Law In The Spiritual World.* In this volume he sought to show through psychology that life can be unified, and that the laws and principles which our inner life reveals enables us to discover also the nature and spirit of God with whom our human lives are bound.

After many years of experiential research, Dr. Jones was able to say assuredly that there are no independent faculties within the inner personal self. He writes: "Perception, conception, memory, imagination, are all interrelated, and are simply varying functions of one common process...."[13] Since this common process within the person is also related to a group life which reaches beyond the circle of the private self, every human life is conjunct with other human lives and with God. In the words of John Donne: "No man is an island, entire of itself; every man is a piece of the continent, a part of the main.... And, therefore, do not ask for whom the bell tolls, it tolls for thee." And when John Woolman reflected on a dream, he came to the important understanding that he "was mixed with" humanity, and that "henceforth (he could) not consider, (himself) as a distinct and separate being." A person cannot be a self alone, nor can God. Professor Jones illustrates:

> Love, if it is to be anything more than a bare abstraction, means that the one who loves, loves somebody, that his life is interrelated with other lives.[14]

Using what he calls "the inward laboratory method," Rufus Jones offers a new meaning to the doctrine of the atonement that is both vital and dynamic:

> It must be put in language which grips the heart, convinces the mind, and carries the will. It will name for us the Divine-human travail for a redeemed humanity. It will cease to signify a way by which God was appeased and it will come to express, as it did in the apostolic days, the identification of God with us in the person of Christ, and the identification, by the power of His love, of ourselves with Him.[15]

And then, in words which characterize the important Quaker contribution of emphasis on the good in humankind, over against their sinful nature, the Professor from Haverford writes:

> Man was not meant for a sinner, and to live a dark, chaotic life. There are far other possibilities in him. He is a potential child of God. The full nature has broken forth in one life and men beheld its glory. 'To as many as receive Him, to them gives He power to become sons of God.'[16]

In 1929, Rufus Jones wrote, "Faith is never ready made; it must be built." An important spiritual discipline used in the building of this faith is prayer — the second half of the double search. This interpreter of the inward way stresses the need to move beyond the "bread and butter" concept of prayer, and see it instead as a way to bring our wills into relationship with God's will. He urges us to move beyond a limited understanding, and see prayer as a calling forth of spiritual power from God. It is more, however, than just receiving, it is spiritual fellowship:

> ... Prayer is spiritual fellowship .... If we could say

nothing more we could at least affirm that prayer, like faith, is itself the victory. The seeking is the finding. The wrestling is the blessing. It is no more a means to something else than love is. It is an end in itself. It is its own excuse for being. It is a kind of first fruit of the mystical nature of personality. The edge of the self is always touching a circle of life beyond itself to which it responds. The human heart is sensitive to God as the retina is to light waves. The soul possesses a native yearning for intercourse and companionship which takes it to God as naturally as the home instinct of the pigeon takes it to the place of its birth. There is in every normal soul a spontaneous outreach, a free play of spirit which gives it onward yearning of unstilled desire.[17]

It is a fact of history that men and women have forever been in search of a Divine Other. The Search has, at times, been shrouded in doubt and sin, but, nevertheless, it continues. We seek to be united with the heart of the universe. We have also discovered, experientially, that our search for God is not a one-way affair, for the God whom we seek is also seeking us. Always he is striving to bring us into union with Him, to lift us to a yet higher spiritual level. Our search for God, and God's search for us, is at the heart of our Christian belief, even though we are living in an age that does not consider the atonement and prayer to be real. This is a serious spiritual problem, and Rufus Jones is able to address this difficulty with a rare sensitivity. These two pillars of our faith rest squarely on the verification of religious experience, and Professor Jones, using his "inward laboratory method," comes to the conclusion that prayer and the atonement are real and are important vehicles in the search for the Divine-human encounter.

Harry Emerson Fosdick, the famous Minister from Riverside Church, New York City, captured the heart of what Rufus Jones wrote by compiling an anthology, entitled, *Rufus Jones Speaks To Our Time*. In the Introduction to this monumental work, Fosdick wrote these reverent words about his beloved friend and teacher:

> Rufus Jones cannot be put into print. He wrote fifty-seven books and uncounted articles and editorials, but even so he himself has never been published. To be sure, one of his friends said about his writings, 'while we are reading them, we feel him near and talking to us in person;' but the man who said that, along with thousands of others who would say the same, had first known Rufus Jones himself. That was a kindling, stimulating experience. He was a radiant person. He possessed the 'inner light' about which he wrote. 'To meet him,' said one of his colleagues, 'was to feel set up for the day.'[18]

Rufus Jones was, indeed, a radiant person whose life was lived as a great adventure of faith, which for him added an important dimension to his total life experience. He believed in the conjunct life, i.e., the world that time and sense have known and the inside workings of the mind with God, make a whole that cannot be separated. All of life, he argued, is an act of faith, since it is the power to see and appreciate and to trust what is still hidden from us. It is to trust that the unseen will complete the seen, and in this faith, Rufus Jones moved and lived, experiencing within his soul the power to see what fulfills and completes what is already available to the outward senses.

Since religion for a Quaker is a seven-day-a-week affair, it cannot be separated and isolated from the rest of life. It is a way of living which effects the whole of existence in attitudes and relationships, supplying a living, transforming power of love through all of life's activities. Rufus Jones was no exception to this general Quaker understanding of religion. One of his pet phrases was, "Living Epistle," which he used to stress the importance of making our lives speak the truth in love as we live out our daily existence in the market place, at home, or in a meeting for worship. Throughout his life, Dr. Jones was a "Living Epistle," sharing through actions instead of rhetoric the meaning of the Gospel message. His life became absorbed in an aim which carried it out of and beyond himself. He will long be remembered, not only as a gifted writer, learned professor, and man of letters, but as one who gave his life, his talent, and his enthusiasm to a presence beyond the physical externalities, to a God of love whom he trusted in absolute faith. It was the deepest purpose of his life to build up again the invisible church within the visible. This spiritual aim was the controlling entity of Rufus Jones' life, and he stands among the landmarks within the Society of Friends, and Christianity as a whole, who pointed the progress of the world along the upward way.

Rufus Jones' interpretation of Christ, the Atonement and Prayer, reveals that he pursued in his life the disciplines of study, service and devotion, which were not isolated from ordinary human experience, but very much a part of it. *The Double Search* combines within its pages depth of thought, clarity in presentation, and a broad spiritual perspective. He writes in the Introduction: "The main feature of this book is its insistence on the facts of experience...."[19] Here is a book, like his many others, which concerns itself with the heart of the Christian faith.

In Elton Trueblood's beautiful Teague Library, where I sit as I write this, there is a picture of Rufus Jones sitting at his desk in his study at Haverford College. He is surrounded by numerous books, many of which he had written himself. I am reminded of how Dr. Jones brought Elton Trueblood to Haverford to be his colleague in the Department of Philosophy, during the last year that Rufus Jones taught. The younger man assisted in the teaching of Jones' famous course in Ethics, which was required of every senior before graduation as a kind of climax of the entire academic experience. It was a course to which students looked forward throughout their college years, and added the finishing touch toward helping them to find a purposeful direction for their lives.

At the home of a friend I have seen a picture of Rufus Jones sitting in front of his summer cottage, Pendle Hill, near China Lake in Maine, surrounded by children from the community. This combination of the Haverford professor and the simple Quaker from Maine, seems, on the surface, to be a contradiction. He was scholarly, a world religious leader, but he never lost touch with his home community. Always he was able to relate to those with whom he was reared. He knew the profound truth that one could be a scholar in religion and philosophy, but if it did not reach into the realm of his daily human experience, it did little good. Thus, his books are based on the facts of human experience, something to which everyone can relate. Such a spirit as Rufus Jones, embodying the boy from New England, the scholar from Haverford, the social activist, and interwoven through all, the Christian mystic, could not help but be a powerful influence on those with whom he came in touch. As numerous as his achievements, however, they were always less than he was. Whoever learns about his deeds as an accomplished author and organizer of the American Friends Service Committee, remember longest the man who did them. He gave people a vision. He writes: "Ever since man was man he has transcended the actual and lived by vision."[20] Such was the life of Rufus Jones. He lived by vision, and he was able to communicate that vision to others. In *The Double Search* he has given us the vision of unending spiritual fellowship with the Living God — He in us, and we in Him.

We are living today in the midst of a smothering spiritual confusion. The Society of Friends is not exempt from this sad state of spiritual affairs. The People called Quakers and Christianity as a whole miss the giant presence of Rufus Jones. His clear distinct message concerning the deeper implications of our time-torn lives is needed as we wander from one ethical crisis to another. Rufus Jones stirred the hearts of thousands of spiritual seekers, and provided reflections from the Light of Christ through his writing, his teaching, his preaching, and his ever present help with questions concerning the religious life. He was a master of words, writing fifty-seven books during his career. Many of these are autobiographical, some historical, but most are volumes dealing with his favorite topic, inner religion and mysticism. The religious scene of today tends to overlook Christian mysticism, and goes, instead, directly to the eastern religions to find the bond of inner peace between the person and God so sought after in our confused world. As a committed Christian, I feel keenly the importance of discovering the words of a man who was Christ-centered, yet mystical. This man is Rufus Jones.

Notes: Chapter IV

[1] Elizabeth Gray Vining, *Friend Of Life* (New York: J.B. Lippincott Co., 1958), p. 262.
[2] Rufus Jones, *A Boy's Religion From Memory* (Philadelphia: Ferris and Leach, 1902), p. 20-21.
[3] Rufus Jones, *Finding The Trail of Life* (New York: The Macmillan Co., 1929), p. 21.
[4] Rufus Jones, *The Eternal Gospel* (New York: Macmillan Co., 1938), p. 105.
[5] Ibid., p. 102.
[6] Rufus Jones, *Practical Christianity* (Philadelphia: The John C. Winston Co., 1899), p. 15.
[7] Daisy Newman, *A Procession of Friends* (Garden City: Doubleday and Co., 1972), p. 6.
[8] Rufus M. Jones, *The Trail Of Life In College* (New York: The MacMillan Co., 1929), p. 129-130.
[9] Ibid., p. 133-134.
[10] Rufus Jones, *New Studies In Mystical Religion* (New York: MacMillan and Co., 1927), p. 186.
[11] Ibid., p. 196-197.
[12] Rufus M. Jones, *The Double Search* (Richmond, Indiana: Friends United Press, 1975), p. 47.
[13] Rufus M. Jones, *Social Law In The Spiritual World* (Philadelphia: John C. Winston Co., 1904), p. 16.
[14] Ibid., p. 17-18.
[15] *The Double Search*, p. 82-83.
[16] Ibid., p. 85.
[17] Ibid., p. 101-102.
[18] Harry Emerson Fosdick, *Rufus Jones Speaks To Our Time* (London: The Bannisdale Press, 1953), p. vii.
[19] *The Double Search*, p. 13.
[20] Ibid., p. 30.

Chapter V

Thomas Kelly: Prophet Of Spiritual Religion

"Few can resist feeling the power of the current that is in this stream."
— Douglas V. Steere

Thomas Kelly was the beloved student of Rufus Jones. While at Haverford during his formative years as a student, Professor Jones became the model which young Kelly sought to emulate. In the words which follow we learn of the older man's deep appreciation for the most popular and lasting work of his prize academician: "I am frequently asked to recommend devotional books. There are a few — a very few great ones, but the list is soon exhausted. Here is a book I can recommend along with the best of the ancient ones. Readers who want spiritual guides will love it and cherish it."[1] *A Testament Of Devotion* is unsurpassed as a spiritual guide because it deals with every major aspect of the inner life. From the first chapter, "The Light Within," to the last, "The Simplification of Life," Kelly takes his readers on a spiritual pilgrimage that leads into the presence of God.

The best way to study the life of this prophet of spiritual religion, is in chapters. His earthly existence can be discerned as a continual quest for truth through the following stages: 1) boyhood and college years at Wilmington, 2) the year of awakening at Haverford, 3) the early searching years of teaching at Wilmington and Earlham, 4) the later years of teaching at Earlham and the University of Hawaii, and 5) the period of "acquaintance with" the Living God.

Thomas Kelly was born near Chillicothe, Ohio, on June 4, 1892. His boyhood years were spent on the farm where he was born, and later in Wilmington, Ohio, where his mother secured a position as a bookkeeper following the death of her husband. Young Thomas' mother decided to move to Wilmington not only because of her job offer, but because there she could ensure for her children a good education at Wilmington College (a Quaker school), and live within the confines of a strong Quaker community.

The boyhood and college years of Thomas Kelly helped to develop his ardent quest for perfection. This quest could be seen in two major areas of interest in his young life — 1) religion and 2) the physical sciences. In *Thomas Kelly: A Biography,* Richard Kelly writes:

> This quest for perfection took forms which competed with each other for all but the last years of his life. The first was a religious interest which stemmed from his earliest years. Even as a little boy on the farm this emphasis was noticeable. The Quaker Meeting and the frequent nearby revivals were the centers of all social life, and he is frequently remembered as having played at being 'minister . . .'

> When, because of bad weather, it was impossible to attend Meeting, it was he who insisted that some sort of service be observed at home. While in college, he was active in the student Y.M.C.A., Christian Endeavor and the Young Friends Movement . . .

> The second aspect of this quest for perfection was a growing love for intellectual inquiry. His grades in elementary and secondary school indicate that he was of exceptional academic ability . . . . At college he majored in chemistry and served as a laboratory assistant in his senior year. 'I loved chemistry,' he wrote some years later, 'and when I get reminded of the old zest of the game I can hardly keep still. A lab

has a smell of its own, and the glitter of blown glass and bottles is as attractive as gold to a miser.'[2]

Thomas Kelly survived these important years of development with a sense of achievement, but not completely. His quest was to continue, and upon graduation from Wilmington College he chose to go east and entered Haverford College in 1913. There he came under the influence of Rufus Jones and became interested in the study of philosophy. His interest in philosophy was natural, since he was able to incorporate both his love for science and his interest in religion into a single area. Rufus Jones writes about Thomas Kelly, the student: "When he was at Haverford as a student... he came to my home deeply moved by his first day's stirring events. He sat down in front of me, his face lighted up with radiance and he said suddenly, 'I am just going to make my life a miracle!' "[3]

Upon completion of his work at Haverford, Thomas Kelly accepted a position teaching science at Pickering College in Canada. Feeling, however, that his life was not yet settled, he decided he wanted to do religious work in the Far East. The idea of doing missionary service in Japan was exciting, so he entered Hartford Theological Seminary to prepare himself for his new ministerial dream. While in seminary he met his wife-to-be, Lael Macy, and was married the day after graduation in 1919. Seminary had put some distance between him and his goal of missionary service in Japan, and after careful thought he decided instead upon a teaching position in the Bible Department at his Alma Mater, Wilmington College. His interest in philosophy was still very much with him, and while in Wilmington he sought an opportunity to study both eastern and western philosophy. This opportunity presented itself in 1921 when Professor A.L. Gillet from Hartford invited him to be his student in philosophy. After three years' work he was granted a Ph.D., but before accepting a position on the faculty at Earlham College, the Kellys went to Germany at the request of the American Friends Service Committee, and there helped in the development of a new kind of Friends Center. This Center was to help in the transition period when the AFSC relinquished control of the German-Child-Feeding Program* into the hands of local German social service agencies.

Thomas Kelly began his tenure at Earlham at the age of thirty-two. His dearest friend while at this prestigious midwestern Quaker school was E. Merrill Root, who writes about Kelly's time while there:

> When I first knew him at Earlham, he was in rebellion against what seemed to him the churchliness or institutionalism of the self-consciously religious; he was a bit brash and brusque, I felt, and a bit too confident of the logical and scientific approach to truth.... He always desired, and more ambitiously in his earlier years, to be a great scholar and to be associated with some college or university that lived by the austere and inexorable standards of excellence in truth which he set for himself. He wished, also and always, to be a living witness of truth; and whenever individuals, or meetings, or colleges, failed to incarnate his passionate desire for truth become flesh, he suffered. He was deeply sensitive and human and wrestled with his disappointments and despairs. He was not wholly happy in his last years at Earlham, because he desired a larger college or university where he could find students of more intense preparation and abilities.[4]

Five years of teaching at Earlham had made Professor Kelly anxious for more academic study, and so he decided in 1930 that he would go to Harvard University. For two years he studied intensely, the highlight being a course taught by Professor Alfred North Whitehead. While taking this course he came in contact with the writings of the French philosopher, Emile Meyerson,

---

*Following the First World War, the AFSC was asked by Herbert Hoover to develop a program that would feed the starving German children. At the time they were asked to do this an estimated one million German children were starving.

and was so impressed with these writings that Emile Meyerson became the topic of his only published book. When Thomas Kelly completed his work at Harvard, he reluctantly accepted back his old teaching position at Earlham. He was not happy about going back, since he had hoped for a position in an eastern school, but one did not become available. In the spring of 1935 an opportunity opened to go to the University of Hawaii and teach philosophy. Douglas Steere writes about the meaning of this move in the Biographical Memoir preceding *A Testament Of Devotion:*

> In the course of that spring an opportunity came to go to the University of Hawaii to teach philosophy and to assimilate what he could of the atmosphere of China and Japan as it was reflected in this curious way-station between Orient and Occident. After a long struggle to decide, he accepted it. It seemed a step into the future again. He wrote Professor Lewis of his reasons for the decision, 'For a number of years I have had a desire to be acquainted with the philosophical thought of the whole world, not merely with the thought of the Western world. To live solely within one's own cultural traditions (in this case, the outgrowths of Greek culture) not actively familiar with the powerful thought of India, China and the rest impresses me as a provincialism not warranted by the spirit of philosophy itself. This point of view was in my mind sometime before I came to Harvard five years ago. And I laid out a tentative and hoped for course of life-development, which had three steps or phases. The first was to get an unimpeachable drill in the most rigorous philosophy department of the West. The second was to get to the Orient, in some way or other, for a period of two, three or four years. (One can hardly comprehend the quest of the Buddha sitting under a maple sugar tree in a mid-west cornfield). The third was to return to this country to teach and write with this world-background.' "[5]

After a year in Hawaii, Thomas Kelly returned to the

mainland, this time to teach at Haverford in a position that was made possible by the departure of D. Elton Trueblood to Stanford. The opportunity provided him with the third phase of life-development for which he had hoped — "to return to this country to teach and write with this world background." The return to Haverford was a happy move for the Kellys, since they were returning to a community of people they knew and dearly loved. With this move came the renewed interest in publishing his work on Emile Meyerson, which was finally printed after Kelly borrowed on his insurance policy to pay for the printing. Thomas Kelly, however, wanted the ultimate scholarly achievement, a Ph.D. degree from Harvard University. After long hours of preparation for his oral exam, he traveled to Cambridge confident and secure in the belief that he would soon be granted his long desired doctorate from Harvard. Richard Kelly relates what happened when his father went up before the board of examiners:

> During the course of the interrogation, Thomas Kelly lapsed into one of his 'woozy spells,' which had been becoming more frequent, and his mind blanked. His performance was so entirely unsatisfactory that he was informed that he would never be permitted to come up for the degree again.[6]

As a result of this let down, the world of Thomas Kelly collapsed. He was so crushed by this defeat that his wife had thought he might take his own life. There was no place to turn except *inward*, and it was as a result of this self-introspection that Thomas Kelly became "acquainted with" the Living Christ. Douglas Steere remembers the change in this Quaker philosopher, and how he was "shaken by the experience of the presence:"

> In the late autumn of 1937 after the publication of his book, a new life direction took place in Thomas Kelly. No one knows exactly what happened, but a strained period in his life was over. He moved toward adequacy. A fissure in him seemed to close, cliffs caved in

and filled up a chasm, and what was divided grew together within him. Science, scholarship, method, remained good, but in a new setting. Now he could say with Isaac Penington, 'Reason is not sin but a deviating from that from which reason came is sin.'[7]

This life changing Divine-Human encounter is discussed in Richard Kelly's book about his father, and he relates his father's experience in this way:

> There is no exact record of what happened in the following weeks, but it is certain that sometime during the months of November or December, 1937, a change was wrought within the very foundation of his soul. He described it as being 'shaken by the experience of the Presence — something that I did not seek, but that sought me.' The inner awakening of an 'Awful Power' surged within him. He later confided to a friend, 'It is an awful thing to give oneself to the Living God.' The Miracle of which he had spoken with such ardor to Rufus Jones so many years before, came in a way he never would have suspected. In the depth of his misery and apparent failure he had found the secret of the pliant spirit as it listens to the interior voice of God. Stripped of his defenses and human self-justification, he found, for the first time, a readiness to accept the outright gift of God's love, and he responded with the unlimited commitment to that leading.[8]

The fifth and final period of life-development was beginning, and now Kelly could clearly see that all that had happened before and all that would come after — all failures and all successes, would be understood by what had happened to him in this final stage of spiritual development. In January of 1938, his new experience would be made manifest in a series of lectures at Germantown, Pennsylvania Friends Meeting. As he spoke, his words were surrounded by the authority of one who had experienced the Living God:

> To you in this room who are seekers, to you, young and old who have toiled all night and caught nothing, but

who want to launch out into the deeps and let down your nets for a draught, I want to speak as simply, as tenderly, as clearly as I can. For God can be found. There is a last rock for your souls, a resting place of absolute peace and joy and power and radiance and security. There is a Divine Center into which your life can slip, a new and absolute orientation in God, a Center where you live with Him and out of which you see all of life, through new and radiant vision, tinged with new sorrows and pangs, new joys unspeakable and full of glory.[9]

The change wrought in Kelly was a radical one. What spiritual power these words bring to us! Here was a man whose life had been completely turned around, a man who moved from "knowledge about" God, to "acquaintance with." The rest of Thomas Kelly's short life would now be spent in total abandon to the Living Christ. He was living proof that radical spiritual change is a possibility, and his testimony adds to the established truth that there is no better verification of God than the experience of persons. St. Augustine said: "Dig deep enough into any man, and you will find something divine." Thomas Kelly had been digging for many years in search for God, and then proved St. Augustine's next great statement: "Thou, O God, hast made us for thyself, and we are restless until we find ourselves in Thee." Although the seeking would continue, as it does in every life on the upward way, Thomas Kelly could also speak of having found, and been found.

It was only through a direct awareness of God that Kelly came to know his true self. He did not attain this knowledge through books or by looking into the mirror, but by an inner mystical experience that is unique. His spiritual life developed through disciplined study, but only when he had reached the slough of despond did he surrender his life completely to the Living God. And then, through an invasion from beyond, Kelly was brought to a sense of exaltation and rapture that would direct his thoughts, words, and actions for evermore. His experience was much like that of Josiah Royce's mother, who made a pioneer journey across the country, and faced many dangers. She writes this account in her *Diary:* "Whence this calm strength which guided me round so surely? .... I had known what it was to *believe* in God and pray that He would never leave us. Now he came so near that I no longer simply believed in Him, but *knew* His presence there, giving strength for whatever might come .... That calm strength, that certainty of One near and all sufficient hushed and cheered me."[10] To believe is different from knowing. Knowledge about is different from acquaintance with, and it was into this later category that Thomas Kelly's life suddenly slipped.

The old despair and negativism of before no longer controlled Kelly's life. Even though he would continue to have some periods of depression, they would no longer be as constant as they had been. He knew now that even though there is an "ocean of darkness," there is also an "infinite ocean of light and life and love that flows over the ocean of darkness." He was now optimistic, and carried within his soul a joy and hope that seemed absent before his conversion. The everlasting arms of God held him, and he was given a sense of ultimate victory and absolute assurance.

When Kelly finally set his feet firmly on the upward way in holy obedience, a powerful message resulted. Appearing first as essays, solicited by editor Elton Trueblood, and published in *The Friend,* these fugitive pieces were collected posthumously and published in a single volume by Harper and Brothers, entitled, *A Testament Of Devotion,* and released in 1941. These essays and addresses were given in the first instance without any thought of them ever being published in a book, or even for the most part, in a magazine. The response to the addresses was, however, such a strong one that requests for publication were made. The people who read the essays, found in volumes 111-114 of *The Friend*, soon recognized that this material was too valuable to be limited to a publication which reached only a small minority of readers. Some of the pressure for publication in book form came not from Quakers themselves, but from Eugene Exman who had already become the highly influential editor of religious books for Harper and Brothers. Mr. Exman's wisdom in this connection is verified by the large numbers of reprintings which constant demand made possible.

It was appropriate for the editor of this classic to place Kelly's thoughts on the fundamental Quaker Principle, "The Light Within," at the beginning. In the following words, this prophet of spiritual religion reveals his understanding of the Inward Christ:

> Deep within us all there is an amazing inner sanctuary of the soul, a holy place, a Divine Center, A speaking Voice, to which we may continuously return. Eternity is at our hearts, pressing upon our time-torn lives, warming us with intimations of an astounding destiny, calling us home unto Itself. Yielding to these persuasions, gladly committing ourselves in body and soul, utterly and completely, to the Light Within, is the beginning of true life. It is a dynamic center, a creative Life that presses to birth within us. It is A Light Within which illumines the face of God and casts new shadows and new glories upon the face of men. It is a seed stirring to life if we do not choke it. It is the Shekinah of the soul, the Presence in the midst. Here is the Slumbering Christ, stirring to be awakened, to become the soul we clothe in earthly form and action. And He is within us all.[11]

With this introduction, Kelly passes through all of the artificial lines of division within Christendom, and speaks a Universal Truth basic to all sects. "And He is within us all." Spiritual religion is synonymous with Basic Christianity, and the fundamental truth of Kelly's words is echoed again and again by others from all denominations throughout Christian history. How often we speak in sectarian terms that do not rest upon a profound experience of Truth. Experiential religion transcends boundaries, since the experiences are basically the same in all times and places. The moving words of St. Francis in his *Little Flowers* could just as easily have been written by a Quaker! Thomas Kelly, and others like him, move us beyond externals to the core of the Christian faith. His purpose is to take his readers beyond the view of a single truth to a wholistic Christian mysticism, and like his teacher, Rufus Jones, he brings us to a level above the world of sects, and ministers to us exclaiming the higher issues of life. He urges us to devote our wills to the Divine Will, and to see the Divine Light penetrating all areas of our living, and not just that little part of us that we save for worship on Sunday morning. This means a more mature understanding of religion, and makes possible a radical transformation in the world. To be at worship within through all of our outward activities, is what Kelly urges for *all* Christians:

> Such practice of inward orientation, of inward worship and listening, is no mere counsel for special religious groups, for small religious orders, for special "interior souls", for monks retired in cloisters. This practice is the heart of religion. It is the secret, I am persuaded, of the inner life of the Master of Galilee. He expected this secret to be freshly discovered in everyone who would be his follower. It creates an amazing fellowship, the church catholic and invisible, and institutes group living at a new level, a society grounded in reverence, history and rooted in eternity, colonies of heaven.[12]

For this prophet of spiritual religion, "The Light Within," is an active energy working *in* us for the complete transformation of our nature. We have often assumed that this possibility existed only for

Saints and Apostles, but not for people like ourselves. Thomas Kelly rejects this presumption on our part, and challenges us to go deeper. To help the individual Christian move into this Divine Center, Kelly discusses the different strata of our mental and spiritual life:

> There is a way of ordering our mental life on more than one level at once. On one level we may be thinking, discussing, seeing, calculating, meeting all the demands of external affairs. But deep within, behind the scenes, at a profounder level, we may also be in prayer and adoration, song and worship and a gentle receptiveness to divine breathings.[13]

Since the world in which we are now living does not cultivate any other strata than just the first, where most of the materialistic business of living is done, anything other than this level is inconceivable to modern man's thought and reasoning. But this does not mean that the more profound level is non-existent. Few things are more impressive than the persistent search of humankind for a deeper level of Divine-Human encounter, and in spite of the excessive effort on the part of humans to secure the tangible goods of earth, Kelly realizes the vital truth that deep down in the heart of every person there is a gnawing hunger for the peace of God. This need for God can be smothered over long periods of time in the confusion of other aims, but, even so, this need will not remain quiet. Every person wants God and the peace that comes from a life founded on an absolute reality, which means, of course, that certain spiritual disciplines must be followed, the most important of which is prayer. But how do we begin a life of "prayer without ceasing?" Thomas Kelly offers some important insight:

> By quiet, persistent practice in turning of all our being, day and night, in prayer and inward worship and surrender, toward Him who calls in the deeps of our souls. Mental habits of inward orientation must be established. An inner, secret turning to God can be made fairly steady, after weeks and months and years

of practice and lapses and failures and returns.[14]

And then, in a bold pronouncement, the mystic from Wilmington challenges his readers to begin NOW:

> Begin now, as you read these words, as you sit in your chair, to offer your whole selves, utterly and in joyful abandon, in quiet, glad surrender to Him who is within. In secret ejaculations of praise, turn in humble wonder to the Light, faint though it may be. Keep contact with the outer world of sense and meanings. There is no discipline in absent-mindedness. Walk and talk and work and laugh with your friends. But behind the scenes, keep up the life of simple prayer and inward worship. Keep it up throughout the day. Let inward prayer be your last act before you fall asleep and the first act when you awake. And in time you will find as did Brother Lawrence, that 'those who have the gale of the Holy Spirit go forward even in sleep.'[15]

As with Hannah Whitall Smith, the *will* is very important in the thought of Kelly. The words that return to the page time and again are, "vigilance," "effort," "Holy Obedience," etc. He warns us in the beginning that this inward life is very difficult, but as we continue to practice the Presence, rewards will be discovered. As time passes our life in the Spirit becomes stronger, but there are times when we regress. These times must be looked upon as opportunities to learn the meaning of forgiveness, and Kelly offers reassurance when this happens:

> Lose no time in self-recriminations, but breathe a silent prayer for forgiveness and begin again, just where you are. Offer this broken worship up to Him and say: "This is what I am except Thou aid me." Admit no discouragement but ever return quietly to Him and wait in His Presence.[16]

A Testament Of Devotion carries little meaning to the person for whom Christianity is first and last a sociological datum. But to those who know the joys and spiritual insights that come from solitude, Kelly's words are intelligible. It was the brilliant Alfred North Whitehead who said: "The great religious conceptions which haunt the imagination of civilized mankind are scenes of solitariness.... Religion is solitariness; and if you are never solitary, you are never religious."[17] Corporate religious activity is important, but so is solitude. Quakers emphasize corporate mysticism, and find these times together to be the basis upon which the spiritual life is built. However, this is not the end of the story! Solitude is also of prime importance in the religious life, and Kelly speaks to this need as few can. As one seeks to move into the deeper levels of life in Christ, finding times when one can be alone with his God is most important.

A paradox soon arises in the life of the spirit as a result of practicing Holy Obedience. In Christ we are set free from the shackles of the world, since we now place our trust in the Divine Center of the universe, and are no longer drawn to materialistic attachments. However, even though we are freed from the world, our concern for the world deepens. Thomas Kelly explains what happens:

> He plucks the world out of our hearts, loosening the chains of attachment. And he hurls the world into our hearts, where we and He together carry it in infinitely tender love.[18]

The biggest mistake of the lone mystic and others who practice complete spiritual isolation is their move away from concern for the world. Kelly preaches a doctrine of otherworldliness, but this in no way should effect our love and concern for the plight of our fellow persons! If anything, the more spiritually developed the seeker becomes, the more concerned he should be for the world. Much of the problem in this regard has come about because of the often extreme emphasis placed on individualism in mysticism. If corporate spiritual expression is not enough, then absolute solitary worship is certainly not enough! In the same way one can forget about his need for solitude, one can also forget about his corporate duty to the world. The cause of wholistic Christian mysticism is not helped by fanatics who are only concerned with the world, or by their counterparts who are only concerned with escape from the world. Kelly seeks a balance in the spiritual life with an equal emphasis on the inner and outer aspects of the total religious experience.

In one of the most beautiful passages to be found in *A Testament Of Devotion,* Thomas Kelly discusses the inner and outer drama taking place in the world today:

> Out in front of us is the drama of men and of nations, seething, struggling, laboring, dying. Upon this tragic drama in these days our eyes are all set in anxious watchfulness and in prayer. But within the silences of the souls of men an eternal drama is ever being enacted, in these days as well as in others. And on the outcome of this inner drama rests, ultimately, the outer pageant of history. It is the drama of the Hound of Heaven baying relentlessly upon the track of man. It is the drama of the lost sheep wandering in the wilderness, restless and lonely, feebly searching while over the hills comes the wiser Shepherd. For His is a shepherd's heart, and He is restless until He holds His sheep in His arms. It is the drama of the Eternal Father drawing the prodigal home unto Himself, where there is bread enough and to spare. It is the drama of the Double Search, as Rufus Jones calls it. And always its chief actor is — the Eternal God of Love.[19]

In viewing life as an inner and outer drama, Kelly places the emphasis on the inner life, which he rightly sees as the place to begin if we are to become concerned with the outer world. He seeks to show that life cannot be explained until persons realize that something more than we *see* is breaking through our life situations and revealing itself. The "chief actor," as Kelly calls him, is working within us to reveal a deeper reality than what our five senses can determine. Holy Obedience means the removal of all barriers that stand in the way of union with the Divine, and this means the surrender of the self. The life of Holy Obedience is the ultimate Christian way of life for which we should strive. Kelly experienced this deep fulfillment, and he offers his readers the same joy and peace:

> The life that intends to be wholly obedient, wholly submissive, wholly listening is astonishing in its completeness. Its joys are ravishing, its peace profound, its humility the deepest, its power world-shaking, its love enveloping, its simplicity that of a trusting child. It is the life and power in which the prophets and apostles lived. It is the life and power of Jesus of Nazareth.... It is the life and power of the apostle Paul, who resolved not to know anything among men save Jesus Christ and Him crucified. it is the life and power of St. Francis.... It is the life and power of George Fox and of Isaac and Mary Penington. It is the life and power and utter obedience of John Woolman, who decided, he says, 'to place my whole trust in God....' It is a life and power that can break forth in this tottering Western culture and return the Church to its rightful life as a fellowship of creative, heavenly souls.[20]

To belong to the "fellowship of creative, heavenly souls," does not just happen. Living in the presence of God is hard work, and Kelly does not want to underestimate this truth. The seeker often thinks that all that is required is a passive mind and a waiting spirit. This is far from true! No one can live in the "fellowship of creative heavenly souls" unless he is ready for the most intense activity, and for the most strenuous life. No person has ever found a rich fulfilling enjoyment of God along paths of least resistance and lazy methods. Holy obedience requires much more. How often the seeker in the spiritual life enters into worship, only to discover that nothing is happening within. Instead of being completely obedient to God, the worshipper catches himself worrying about a squabble at work, or who will play in the Super Bowl! The mind is a marvelous instrument and capable of much wandering. The goal in worship is to get the mind to wander in the region which ministers to the spiritual life, for it is in this realm where the work of the Spirit is done. In Holy obedience, Thomas Kelly was able to turn his attention to the deeper level of the Spirit, so that he became a person possessed with the eternal presence.

For Thomas Kelly, this eternal possession was greatly intensified following his return from Germany in 1939. This mission to Europe had taught him a new meaning of suffering, since on this trip he had been "stained with sorrow's travail." The German experience was a life changing one, as he shared with his mother before returning home: "I am not at all as I was when I came to Germany, as you will find when you see me." With the vividness of his European trip in mind, Kelly was able to share at a deeper level the true meaning of suffering:

> One returns from Europe with the sound of weeping in one's ears, in order to say, 'Don't be deceived. You must face Destiny. Preparation is only possible now. Don't be fooled by your sunny skies. When the rains descend and the floods come and the winds blow and beat upon your house, your private dwelling, your own family, your own fair hopes, your own strong muscles, your own body, your own soul itself, then it is well-nigh too late to build a house. You can only go inside what house you have and pray that it is founded upon the Rock. Be not deceived by distance in time or space, or the false security of a bank account and an automobile and good health and willing hands to work. Thousands, perhaps millions as good as you have had all of these things and are perishing in body and, worse still, in soul today.'

...One comes back from Europe aghast at having seen how lives as graciously cultured as ours, but rooted only in time and property and reputation, and self-deluded by a mild veneer of religious respectability but unprepared by the amazing life of commitment to the Eternal in holy obedience are now doomed to hopeless despair. For if you will accept as normal life only what you can understand, then you will try only to expel the dull, dead weight of Destiny, of inevitable suffering which is a part of normal life, and never come to terms with it or fit your soul to the collar and bear the burden of your suffering which must be borne by you, or enter into the divine education and drastic discipline of sorrow, or rise radiant in the sacrament of pain. The heart is stretched through suffering, and enlarged. But O the agony of this enlarging of the heart, that one may be prepared to enter into the anguish of others! Yet the way of holy obedience leads out from the heart of God and extends through the Valley of the Shadow.[21]

To "enter into the anguish of others" is the responsibility of all who want to be Holy obedient, and Thomas Kelly saw this as one important gateway to the Eternal. More than anything else in his life this experience taught him about the sinful nature of humankind. In affirming the "Light Within," Kelly in no way saw this as an exaltation of self, since he freely acknowledged the corrupt nature of persons. Germany greatly intensified this understanding. He never allowed, however, his realistic exposure to sin to bring him to the conclusion that there is no good within persons. Instead, he was able to maintain a mutual tension between a naive optimism about human nature, and a crippling pessimism. In this way he was true to the early Quaker understanding of the "Light," about which Hugh Barbour has written in his book, *The Quakers In Puritan England.* He says Early Friends understood the "Light" at first as a source of terror rather than hope. "The essence of pain was to know one's sins and self will, but the source of the pain was the Light, itself."[22]

Kelly was never tempted to speak naively about the goodness of human nature, without coupling with it an emphasis on the evil of persons. Germany was a time of maturing, and he returned to this country radically changed, since he had been brought face to face with evil, which only intensified his effort to seek the God of love. The "Light Within," had brought him to the reality of sin, but it had also enabled him to move beyond sin, to the vision of perfection. He knew that the concept of perfectionism is essentially a paradox, for it is wrong to say you have acquired it, and it is equally wrong to deny its possibility. Mystics are *realists* and *visionaries,* and Thomas Kelly exemplified this definition perfectly.

In the beautiful words which follow, this prophet of spiritual religion concludes *A Testament Of Devotion* by sharing the meaning of a life lived from the Center:

> Life from the Center is a life of unhurried peace and power. It is simple. It is serene. It is amazing. It is triumphant. It is radiant. It takes no time, but it occupies all our time. And it makes our life programs new and overcoming. We need not get frantic. He is at the helm. And when our little day is done we lie down quietly in peace for all is well.[23]

This masterpiece of Christian devotion cannot be easily classified within the general classifications of spiritual literature. It is not a journal, nor is it an autobiography. It is not a collection of prayers and meditations, stories, or allegories. So where does it belong? Under what genre of devotional literature can we place it? The term *testimony* seems to apply, and is distinct from these other forms of description. In it we capture the mind of a man whose spiritual life grew through mental suffering, and matured through disciplined study. It is dateless, and is not an exercise in reason *about* the religious life, but is, instead, a testimony *of* the religious life. Although it has not gone through the rigors of the years like Penn's *Fruits Of Solitude*, or Woolman's *Journal*, it can still rightly be called a "Classic." No one before Kelly, or after, has put so many beautiful, helpful words into a devotional testimony.

From time to time in the history of the world, there are men and women who are especially rich in the things of the Spirit, persons who live their lives around an Orienting Center. They do not find words capable of expressing their experience, but when they do share as best they can through the printed page, we are lifted into the vision of a new and exciting existence. Thomas Kelly is one of these persons, and his *Testament of Devotion* is a moving account, revealing to us how we can enter into the same kind of relationship with God that he experienced. This prophet of spiritual religion belonged to that company of souls who shared a oneness with God, and it was his desire to bring all who sought God into this higher region.

The mystics have always had their "dark nights of the soul," when God seemed absent following earlier revelatory experiences, and preceding a time of peace within the soul. The darkness through which Thomas Kelly fought his troubled way was not of this sort. His quest was through a continuous shadow, never fully experiencing the Living Presence of Christ until his last visit to Germany. He found little help from his material life, which seemed only to deepen his misery, and friends could not speak to his tormented condition. But beneath the seemingly hopeless surface, a seed broke forth! Thomas Kelly wore through his darkness, the clouds finally began to break away, and the "glorious Dayspring from on high" arose upon him.

Thomas Kelly died much too early, at the age of 48, on January 17, 1941. The struggles through which he fought his troubled way can all be seen as a search for the Divine, at first through science and philosophy. The perfect "reason" was his goal. In the end, however, he discovered that his vast amount of knowledge was of little help in his personal spiritual pilgrimage. He discovered, following his defeat before the Harvard examiners, that "our knowledge is imperfect." But out of this defeat in the eyes of men, came a victory in the sight of God. His life of mysticism was born out of human failure, as is so often the case, for it is in the depths of despair, where we find ourselves utterly incompetent, that we finally turn to God. When we yield ourselves to Him, as Thomas Kelly did, we find the Inward Christ patiently waiting to welcome us home.

The duty of Thomas Kelly, like that of the other four writers of these Quaker Classics, is to lift us to higher visions of our human potential, to greater hopes for our world, and to more profound expressions of encounter with the Living Christ. Once having taken us to the inward spring, these servants of spiritual religion are not able to make us drink, but they do make the fountain of inner devotion more accessible to those who thirst for the Living Water of experiential religion. By the living of their lives and the recording of their experiences, these shepherds of Basic Christianity have shown us a deeper dimension into which our lives can slip. If they can point us to a level of experience that transcends the outward elements of time and sense, and change lives because of their changed lives, then their God-given task will have been accomplished, and this volume will have helped to serve this purpose.

These champions of inward religion are with us no more, but they have left a part of themselves in the form of their great books. Their physical presence is missed, but their spiritual insights shall forever be shedding new light on our human condition. None of these giants knew that they were writing a classic when they undertook their respective literary tasks, since, on the whole, "genius is ever a secret to itself." But as the years passed and the printed word became more and more a vehicle of sharing ideas, these volumes stood out from the rest of the mass of literature as possessing truth. Truth, as mentioned in the Preface to this volume, is independent of the time when it is produced. Nothing makes literature so mortal as to reflect the period in which it is written, for if a writer marries his age, he will be a widower in the next. A classic is born when it withstands the vagaries of vogue, and shares truth regardless of time. These volumes have withstood the challenge of time, and are assured of loving companionship for ages to come. They have taken their rightful place on the shelf reserved for the classics of religious literature.

Notes: Chapter V

[1] Thomas Kelly, *A Testament Of Devotion* (New York: Harper and Brothers, 1941), Front Cover.
[2] Richard Kelly, *Thomas Kelly: A Biography* (New York: Harper and Row, 1966), p. 23-24.
[3] *A Testament Of Devotion*, p. 3.
[4] Ibid., p. 6.
[5] Ibid., p. 12-13.
[6] *Thomas Kelly: A Biography*, p. 90.
[7] *A Testament Of Devotion*, p. 18.
[8] *Thomas Kelly: A Biography*, p. 91-92.
[9] *A Testament Of Devotion*, p. 18-19.
[10] *A Frontier Lady* (Yale Press, 1932).
[11] *A Testament Of Devotion*, p. 29.
[12] Ibid., p. 32-33.
[13] Ibid., p. 35.
[14] Ibid., p. 38.
[15] Ibid., p. 38-39.
[16] Ibid., p. 39.
[17] Alfred North Whitehead, *Religion In The Making* (New York: The MacMillan Co., 1926), p. 17, 19.
[18] *A Testament Of Devotion*, p. 47.
[19] Ibid., p. 51.
[20] Ibid., p. 54-55.
[21] Ibid., p. 69-71.
[22] Hugh Barbour, *The Quakers In Puritan England* (New Haven & London: Yale University Press, 1964), p. 98.
[23] *A Testament Of Devotion*, p. 124.